PRAISE FOR *WHAT'S HAPPENING TO US?*

Miller's perception of the baby boomer male persona is so close to home, I laughed until I cried. His anatomy of "Midlife Crisis" was a direct hit to the head and heart. No shrinks needed here. Extremely explicit yet inspirational reading for both sexes. *J. Paul*

OMG. Women may have suspected, but really have no idea about what goes on inside the male head. The chapters literally put you into the brain of a typical man through the aging and maturation stages of his life. Every woman who sincerely wants a better understanding of their relationship needs to read this book. *Melissa M.*

Completely honest and deadly clear. Most men think this stuff, but social pressure has made them too afraid to say it out loud. Up until I finished this book, I never really thought about how Testosterone had such an impact on my words, thoughts and actions. Locker room talk supreme!! Whew! Glad he said it, not me.... *Roger P.*

This book is timely, unfailingly honest and very funny. For all of us that survived the sixties, seventies and eighties, it reflects on how men viewed their women. The last few chapters are a bible that can help all boomers share the love and care they'll need as hormones ebb. A blueprint that love for each other and life can conquer all. *Sandra B.*

A male revolution? A Germaine Greer for men? Let's go pump some iron and eat nails. The author's take on "our hero" tells it like it was and how it is now. Inspiring and warm, while all the time keeping it real right up until the end. *Allan H.*

WHAT'S HAPPENING TO US?

HOW THE QUEST FOR EQUALITY HAS ERODED COMMUNICATION AND CONNECTEDNESS IN OUR RELATIONSHIPS

REGG MILLER

Clovercroft Publishing

What's Happening to Us?

©2018 by Regg Miller

Published by Clovercroft Publishing, Franklin, Tennessee

Senior Editor: Tammy Kling

Assistant Editor: Tiarra Tompkins

Copy Editor: Christy Callahan

Cover Designer: Sarah Thurstenson

Interior Designer: Suzanne Lawing

Printed in the United States of America

ISBN: 978-1-948484-29-9

This book is dedicated to the two most influential women in my life: my mother Molly (who left us and is surely in heaven) and my wife, Teresa. I can only admire the patience and respect the unconditional love they showered me with in spite of the unrelenting and unforgiving demands "Mr. T" heaped on my maleness throughout the years.

> **For women who really want to understand their men**

CONTENTS

INTRODUCTION

THE SKINNY

Have most men forgotten to be men? I find myself asking this question more frequently than ever.

Let me begin by saying that this book will not be an easy read for some, and I never intended for it to be. I share many of my personal views and stories—some will call them rants—which many will label as harsh and a prime example of male chauvinism. I have no doubt, throughout the course of this book that I will piss off more than a few women, and maybe some men too. But I say, let the chips fall where they may. Ultimately, this is a book about personal responsibility, and I hope that it encourages both men and women to take responsibility for living the lives they've chosen and that they will find peace, compassion, and contentment in the company of each other as the years roll by.

You're a man, the strongest sex of the species. Right? Well, maybe not if your boss is a woman, or if she earns the big bucks in the household. If you find yourself in that position, are you living a Jekyll and Hyde life? Do you habitually bite your tongue, suppress your thoughts, look away from attractive women? Do you hang out in gyms, locker rooms, golf courses, pay-per-view arenas, or other places in order to find comfort from guys who think like you?

For the old boys' club, it seems like that's the way it's going. So it begs the question, Are men losing the ability to be real men? Has our society put the kibosh on testosterone-influenced behavior? Are we on the threshold of a redefinition of the sexes? Do women even need men in the future?

Women used to adhere to the understanding that they should be seen and not heard. In fact, it's still that way today in many foreign countries, but not here. In North America, it's become the opposite. Since men have allowed this "equality," they are now the ones who must be wary of their actions both verbally and physically while liberated women take over as CEOs, Supreme Court justices, and politicians. The pendulum has swung 180 degrees.

Let's break it down. Every guy out there knows all too well about estrogens and progesterone, PMS, menopause, yeast infections, hot flashes, age lines, Botox, liposuction—the list goes on. Oh yes, we see all those female commercials enlightening us on why it is imperative for women to keep up their youthful appearance. Make no mistake about it; women have crammed these issues down our throats by crying, "Men will never understand the ongoing issues that aging women have to deal with." Maybe that's true, but so is this: Men have their own set of hormones, anger, and frustrations. And women who want better relationships need to open their minds and hearts to our problems as well.

If the goal is equality of the sexes, then there must be room for men to be heard as well. Wouldn't you agree?

Women have taken equality too far. Women are getting bolder, and although we love them and can't do without them, there needs to be some balance between the sexes. Accept it or not, our men have been the acquiescing catalyst for allowing both ethnic and sexual equality in our society, so why are they suffering so much? Truth is, women have been allowed to flourish because those same men have backed off and encouraged them to do their thing. A fine point? Well, check out women's freedoms and status on other continents and convince me it's not so. Our men have stood behind their word to champion equality; it's earned them a feather in the quiver of "should be appreciated more" and a true testament of testosterone management.

This book observes Mr. T's influence in the chronological and mental development over a typical man's lifetime as well as how the "King of hormones" weighs on his relationships. Life begins simple enough, then ratchets through the turbulent years of lusting, loving, and hunting for material supremacy, trending in later years toward a calmer, more loving future after testosterone settles down. Once child-rearing is out of the way, a couple of questions linger: Will our women even need men as they become more independent and powerful? Or will men and women walk hand and hand into the sunset of life forever at odds, but in love?

CHAPTER 1

A LITTLE HISTORY

Over the last half-century, the push for sexual equality in North America has propelled us into a predicament. This push threatens the very nature of men, which is "the provider/protector/procreator." It touches the once-dominant characteristics innately woven into the human male. If you're a woman reading this, you may find it difficult to hold back while you witness the early years. Do not be influenced by those harsh realities; rather, get to the mid-years before passing final judgment.

Have you noticed that for the last several decades, women have thrown "feminine" issues in their men's faces and demanded we understand their physical and mental composition? Perhaps it's time to put the shoe on the other foot. You will have to remember that this book is skewed to a specific male point of view. Nothing personal, political, or sexually correct here, just the facts, ma'am. We can agree on facts, right?

HAVE YOU NOTICED THAT FOR THE LAST SEVERAL DECADES, WOMEN HAVE THROWN "FEMININE" ISSUES IN THEIR MEN'S FACES AND DEMANDED WE UNDERSTAND THEIR PHYSICAL AND MENTAL COMPOSITION?

Historically, women acted as "the helpers," supporting the man by managing the tasks at home and raising the offspring, while he would hunt and face dangerous animals, terrain, and weather. We are all aware that the traditional role of women has since changed over the last few centuries. What caused those changes?

In our North American society, compared to all other societies around the globe, women have made massive strides in their social, sexual, and political status. Those gains have rewarded them with many "stereotypically male" jobs. This has placed the successful corporate women side by side after work with the boys in bars and clubs where they try to unwind from the stress of success. And it doesn't stop there.

Currently, our women are not only at our sides; they are also the ones who have taken the reins and are surging into the corporate breach. There is a lot of anger out there. There's confusion, reward, sacrifice, and satisfaction from both sexes. Men are trying to bravely go forward, competing head-to-head with the fairer sex, but the rules of engagement have been skewed sharply in the female favor. Just as equality of race has set up reverse discrimination of Caucasians, men of all races have suffered as society demanded that women be given equal opportunity. This has crossed all lines in the job force, political arenas, and even the military. And so it goes.

The purpose of this book is to look at how men have historically viewed the world, versus their current perception. Let's clear up one perception first, which is men have always wanted their mate to share and have all the opportunity he had. But as in most visions, the premise is flawed, not because those goals are too far out there, but because we start out at polar ends of the spectrum. Genetics writes certain characteristics into each identity. Even so, we have thrown these male and female differences into a blender, expecting more or less an equal outcome.

It once was a man's world; now the dividing line is not so clear as it was to our ancestors. We've become an androgynous society of compromising workaholics. Our families and friends are caught in this elusive mouse trap too. How come no one told us our lives were supposed to be so tough, so long, and so unforgiving?

Women who can get past the male bias will find this book a portal into the heart of their men. Likewise, sharing the contents of the following pages with the man you live with and love may help you understand the confusion he deals with on a daily basis. God knows most women don't even want to go anywhere near the stigma of testosterone, but in order for our society to evolve with harmony, women must learn to accept the fact that it's in us and we are sensitive too. It's time for women to let men be men once again.

For too long our society and strong women have told us men point-blank, "Take it like a man," "Real men don't cry," "You call yourself a man?"—even "What kind of man are you?" The operative word "man" in all these expressions seems to put some kind of "one-dimensional thickness" on us. As if we could snap our fingers or take the "man" pill to create the perfect environment where sexual, physical, and mental equality magically appears in both sexes. We all know this will never be the case.

These clichés have been the battle shrill of the male species for eons. But because of progressive education, those same men are now cornered and coerced to accept and be sensitive to female imbalances, hormones, etc. Up till now, it's been the men who have had to open up and try hard to understand the crosses women bear. That experience has pretty much been a one-way street. It's about time our women acknowledge and understand the effects male hormones have on their men.

Every guy out there knows all too well about estrogen and progesterone, PMS, menopause, yeast infections, hot flashes, age lines, Botox, liposuction, etc. Oh yes, we see all the prescription drugs on all those female commercials enlightening us. Countless movies and TV shows satirize women's so-called "moodiness." The audiences chock it up to the menstrual cycle, hormonal imbalance, and even to menopause. But make no mistake about it—women have crammed these issues down our throats by crying, "Men don't have to deal with these things. You'll never understand."

There's no fair play here. If we mention testosterone (most women all know about this one) or androgens (not so many know about that one), we get the "Oh, please" or an eye roll and we are virtually dismissed. Men are just told to deal with their issues.

> IF WE CAN ALL AGREE ON THE NOTION THAT EQUALITY IS THE GOAL BETWEEN THE SEXES, THEN FOR EQUALITY TO EARN ITS NAME, EACH SIDE MUST MAKE AN EFFORT TO UNDERSTAND HOW THE OPPOSITE GENDER IS BUILT AND NOT JUST THEIR OWN.

Doesn't that seem slightly tilted?

If we can all agree on the notion that equality is the goal between the sexes, then for equality to earn its name, each side must make an effort to understand how the opposite gender is built and not just their own. Presently, I think it's safe to say women are lagging behind here. Sharing the knowledge of functions and genetics will only help bridge the obvious disparity between men and women. More than ever, this convergence is necessary, so that as we age, we can care for and love each other in the way we were designed. There's no doubt that as our hormones recede and fade to black, we will have to depend on each other for quality of life. Quite simply, we must forge forward and enter a new era of mutual understanding based on both sexes if we want to be together.

***

Three or four thousand years ago, the average lifespan was under thirty. Birth, adolescence, mating, and death were clearly defined segments of human existence. There were no grandchildren, retirement, or extended health care plans to deal with at that time.

As we push deeper into the twenty-first century and life expectancies balloon well into the eighties, nineties, and the century mark, we're forced to coexist in a world where our initial function of procreation becomes irrelevant. At this point, we have to wonder, are we outliving our purpose? Good question, because nowadays great-, great-great-, and even great-great-great-grandchildren are becoming very much the norm.

All these extra years have added new dimensions and needs to our species, and it's happened in a historical blink of an eye. When you throw the rapid rate of medical and technical breakthroughs into the mix, humans have never had so much to be thankful for or baffled by.

What are some of the issues the male gender faces with longevity now at play? Let's start the education process by first noting one huge dilemma for man. Before, during, and after the years spent raising a family, a man must to learn how to manage his testosterone. As he enters his post-reproductive years, the amount of this hormone begins to decrease. However, the hunter and his sexual appetite (even if it's only in his mind) never dies. It's innate in him until the end. This book takes a stab at how men deal with the continual injection of testosterone into his cellular makeup from birth to death. To his credit, the book sheds light on how our misunderstood hero manages this raging baby tiger through his years of lust, love, sex, and relationships.

CHAPTER 2

THE SITUATION: WOMEN ABSOLUTELY KNOW THIS

In nearly every species around the globe except humans, the male and female roles are defined and permanent. Markings or physically distinguishing traits make it easy for each sex to identify the other sex, connect, and mate. From birds to bees, from mice to ducks, from elephants to zebras, from cheetahs to gazelles, all is in order. There is competition of course, but little confusion. After all, what would gay kangaroos or lesbian penguins accomplish? Easy! No offspring and the species would die off quickly. Humans aren't that lucky.

We are the progressive species, right? So what has happened to us as members of the Hominidae (primate) superfamily—taxonomically *Homo sapiens*, which in Latin means "wise man" or "knowing man"? It started out okay, then poof, it got all screwed up. Humans were empowered and created a couple of things that other species don't have: namely, superior problem-solving brains (we got too wise for our own good) and a mortgage. And when men started inventing ways to make things easier, those sex-defining roles deviated and evolved to where we are today.

Unlike our animal counterparts that only worry about food, shelter, being eaten, and seasonal mating, we became hell-bent on amassing possessions and wealth. To add to the confusion, we made sex a year-round activity. Basically, we got bored and started screwing everyone, both monetarily and physically. Sex and manipulation for money became the pastime of choice, right up there with a good book or a long sermon. And as time went speeding by, we needed more toys to keep us happy.

Enter the nail in the coffin. Cash flow is the serial killer of our species. Some madman made the fatal mistake of creating money. That led to a stock market, vibrant economies, and supreme greed. Now we live in houses—the bigger, the better—and buy luxury SUVs and 80-inch 4K TVs and pay for ridiculous services from gardening and pool maintenance to internet and our kids' private education. The list goes on ad infinitum.

How did the almighty dollar influence sex? Once man could buy and sell it at his disposal, and women could make a living from it, it blurred the lines. There was a foggy distinction between love, lust, passion, infidelity, prostitution, arranged marriages, and all the other forms that money controlled. This muddying of the water is another factor that threw the wrench into the gears of sexual distinction and dysfunction.

Add to the mix, advances in technology that continually upgraded our lifestyle and caused more segregation for the sexes. And if we didn't find love on the opposite side of the fence, we looked around on the same side. It may have started in San Francisco, down near the wharf (just joking), but it quickly made its way from Atlantic to Pacific. Of course, once gay rights hit Hollywood and the main streets of Boston, we were cooked. But we're getting away from the main topic, so for argument's sake, we're going to stick to the majority, the hetero world.

As our society marched on into the modern era, inventions and lawyers dominated growth. With this creation of wealth and power, males were set free from the tedium of labor and that led to even more easy sex. Along this path, we most certainly fought like hell to achieve liberation. And it wasn't too long before we got our wish. Disposable income let us do pretty much whatever we liked. Over the years, this included going to war, being jealous, screwing the babes you liked, and sticking it to the ones you didn't. It also set in motion the phrase "keep up with the Joneses."

We've all thought to ourselves at some point that we want a better version of something we already have. Think of the last thing you upgraded. Each generation from the 1940s on created more wealth, more fashion, more industry—more and more, bigger and better. And why not bathe yourself in available luxury? A better thingamajigger, a smaller, faster computer, a wider HD TV, a

> THUS, MEN AND WOMEN WANT IT ALL, PERIOD. SO WHEN THE SHIT HIT THE FAN, THE MEN STARTING SCREAMING, "HONEY, CAN YOU HELP ME OUT WITH THE BILLS?"

new Android or iPhone, a six-bedroom oceanside villa with

an Olympic-sized swimming pool, a sexier body, better skin, a younger face. Name your desire and our capitalist society will make it happen. But at what price?

You see, all these miracles come with a dollar attachment. (There is no such monetary or vanity equivalent in the animal kingdom.) Thus, men and women want it all, period. So when the shit hit the fan, the men starting screaming, "Honey, can you help me out with the bills?"

***

During the nineteenth century, the arriving settlers at the time were generally decent and appreciative toward women. They laid down their jackets so the ladies wouldn't get their shoes muddy, opened doors, lit cigarettes, took their hats off, and stood up at a table every time a woman did out of respect. Chivalry was alive and well.

Men respected the softer, gentler sex and truly competed for them sexually and to become their partners. Women were highly revered, yet they longed for so much more. As we entered the twentieth century, society's goals got loftier and more expensive. Naturally, women wanted all those nice things too. However, during and after the Second World War when most of the men were off fighting, women stepped up to the plate. When the boys returned and couldn't afford luxury, heaven bless the young women who were willing to chip in. The dual-income family was born, and a whole new set of values took over.

Fast-forward to today. Why are the most popular and profitable shows on television *Desperate Housewives, America's Next Top Model, The Bachelor/Bachelorette, Sex in the City, The Golden Girls, Oprah, The Ellen DeGeneres Show, AM Joy,* and all soap operas? Because women watch and support these TV programs in droves. Why do women's retail stores outnumber men's six to one and have five times more floor space in department stores? Because the men in charge needed ways to make money. They knew women love fashion and were willing to spend their man's money on looking pretty. Why are makeup or jewelry counters at or near the entrance of every major department store? Because women want to smell and look good! Is it only for themselves or to attract men? Is the opposite true about men?

Well, let's take a look. Why are the Super Bowl, NBA, World Cup, NHL playoffs, MMA, boxing, and the World Series so popular and profitable? Because men watch and support these events in droves.

Do men participate in the former and women the latter? Of course, but in much, much smaller percentages. Is there a pattern here? Women browse the shops; men browse the sports channels. Women buy makeup; men buy watches. Women like putting on a dress and going out. Men throw on blue jeans and wash their cars. So what's the connection? Are men watching football or boxing to attract women? Surely, you jest.

> THIS POSES A GREAT QUESTION: WHAT *DO* WOMEN WANT FROM THEIR MEN?

This poses a great question: What *do* women want from their men?

In spite of the glaring differences, men like women and women like men. The vast majority not only want to be in each other's company, but they both also want to fall hopelessly in love and live happily ever after. So why do these opposites fatally attract? Simple! It's Biology 101. We've been given the task to procreate and prolong our species just like every other animal, fish, insect, and reptile on this planet. Women are the wide receivers (they got the eggs), men are the quarterback passers (they throw the sperm). Fact is, until this changes, there aren't any other options. By and large, the fertilization of that screaming bundle of joy is attained by sexual intercourse, and we, as a nation, are consumed by "the old in and out" during our active reproductive years. So that solves the mystery of why we attract, period.

> HERE'S A FACT MOST WOMEN DON'T UNDERSTAND.

But what happens when jobs, debts, lines of credit, and diapers become the priority? What pressures hit the natural state of male/female roles when children arrive? What happens to the relationship after mating "season" is over?

Here's a fact most women don't understand. Every man who's ever been smitten by Cupid's arrow would love to give his princess everything she could ever ask for in life. In a perfect and traditional world, she wants to be pampered and treated with cuddles and respect. He'd love to do that. She wants diamonds and pearls and a beautiful home complete with a huge walk-in closet and shoe wall, a double sink with vanity mirror in the bathroom, and a bidet. He'd love to give that too. She wants to be loved, made love to, have earth-shattering orgasms, and be put on a pedestal. Then after a couple of years, she wants to have great kids and be a great-grandmother down the road. He'd be the happiest man on earth, if he could supply these things (especially the earth-shattering "Os").

She doesn't want to worry about finances and hardships—that's a man's job. He'd be happy to take those problems away too. She doesn't want to take out the garbage, cut the grass, fix the car, or have to reprimand the kids. He's down with that as well. I think this Chinese proverb sums it up: "Happy wife, happy life." It's true, a man in love would move the world for his woman. Unfortunately, these fantasies are too far out of the normal man's budget. So her dreams are just dreams that don't ever actualize. A man can only do what he's capable of, and six or seven figure incomes are few and far apart.

Sounds too familiar, am I right, guys?

A large majority of women will never experience the true lap of luxury her man would love to afford her, because with or without a husband/partner, she's trying just as hard to make ends meet. She is overwhelmed with raising children, working the job, shopping, cleaning, contributing to the relationship, and chauffeuring the kids to their activities while trying to keep her man occupied with some kind of sex life. It's a multitasking nightmare. By the way, don't think your guy is oblivious to your timetable, hormonal imbalances, and stress levels—he's very aware of those mood swings, but he's got his internal struggles, sex drive, and the crankiness that goes along with his hormones too.

Continuing with the plight of our women, if she's reduced into a single-parent role, because her a-hole husband took off with the young secretary, the task is twice or thrice as hard. But it's not only women who are faced with adversity, and it's not always the man's fault. Remember, it takes two to tango and two to argue. So what about the boys?

Well, a disgruntled portion of the male population has fallen from the ranks of the main breadwinner. This is because some women are better at the job than he is. So Mr. Arrogant has tumbled to Mr. Humble Pie, thereby losing his self-esteem. Now he gets to do all the traditionally female things at home while Mrs. Corporate earns the dough. This is a tough pill to swallow, and the verdict is still out on whether either of them is comfortable with it, but he's willing to give it a shot, while she's out there doing her thing.

Ironically, our female provider ends up having a few pints at the end of the day just like the boys. She's gotta release the stress in the corporate world of vicious competition too. All about getting ahead, getting the best, being one up, and so on.

Thus, in these instances, both sexes have flip-flopped into less identifiable categories with unparalleled indefinable characteristics that have all the shrinks at a loss for solutions. Is the last sentence too complicated, too ambiguous just like our lives? Is there any hope?

Right from the dawn of history, men and women had a completely different set of hormones dedicated to specific tasks. Among others, men have testosterone. It is the preferred hormone for killing and mating. Basically, they hunt, provide, and kill what they eat or whatever gets in the way of having random sex.

Among others, women have oxytocin, the cuddle hormone, a key to pair bonding. Here's a typical way each sex sees the relationship unfolding.

Woman: First date, he's passable and gets a kiss on the cheek. Second date, he's a lot better and gets the open mouth and tongue. Third date, she offers herself sexually. And from that point on she's looking long term.

Man: First date, she's interesting, but turned so I'd kiss her on the cheek. Second date, she's looking better and let me suck her tongue. I'm going to give her one more chance to get laid or I'm moving on. Third date, I do get laid, and we'll see how it goes, but I could be ready to move on anyway.

Simply put. Men want to have sex and see what's next.

Women want to have sex and grow a family. Of course, this is oversimplifying each case, but in the beginning, this was pretty much it. Through evolution and revolution, we have reached critical mass, as both sexes seek a new and more profound place. So what's going to happen? One thing's for sure: There will be sex and copious amounts of it. We're just not sure who will be seducing who or who's on top.

Good luck to us all because the next generation has no idea how this will play out. From professionals to plain people on the street, there is massive concern about where the line in the sand will be drawn or where each sex will end up.

Hope things round out soon 'cause there's a lot of resentment out there amid the muted thoughts and ambiguous words of our leaders. Trump, is the very latest example of "deny, deny, deny" while accusing all women of lying, as he's supporting men who've been accused of sexual harassment to domestic violence. With this kind of ambivalence, it's no wonder the "me too" movement will only expand and ultimately succeed. Although more than half the human race is women, this book deals with how a majority of North American men feel and think about their plight in the twenty-first century. If women go through the exercise of understanding how and why men were created, how they are raised and how they mature, then surely by putting our heads together, we can solve the mystery of where testosterone will fit into the future. Don't forget ladies, there are amounts of "Mr. T" in you too; it helps keep your bones and muscles strong. During the turbulent pages of this book, we're asking both sexes to be sensitive to our newfound search for "equality."

CHAPTER 3

THE DILEMMA

North American men are in the most profound battle since they set foot on this new land's soil. It's not in Afghanistan ... or Iraq, Iran, or North Korea. It's not competing in the beds of ultra-rich oil barrens who indiscriminately fornicate with any women they desire because money is never an object.

No, it's right here at home, and it threatens the singularly most male trait we were born with. What is it you ask? Well, are we witnessing "live," the subtle, gradual erosion of "Real Men" and the hormone that has punctuated maleness since Adam did Eve: namely, testosterone.

The layman's version would simply be: Are men losing their balls?

Testosterone ("Testy," "T," or "Mr. T"), the kill-something or seduce-someone hormone, has reached a derisive juncture in mainstream manhood. In today's society, we are not at ease to randomly kill, and all sex must be consensual. We've gone to great lengths, at great expense creating courts and laws to prohibit that kind of barbaric behavior. However, T was inserted into man's genes specifically to accomplish both. Mr. T typically exhorts the kind of male characteristics we all love. You know the ones. Dominant, chauvinistic, competitive, boorish, horny, aloof, overbearing, cold, uncaring, etc.

The main point is that men are being nudged (not always against their will) through sociological pressures to suck it up and be fair, nice, and compassionate, to think before speaking, and a host of other subduing tactics that are retrofitting our psyche to a more compliant being.

Let's examine the massive pressure being exerted to make him submit. He is continually being called out on how to blend in without offending society's values. We all know today's pseudo civilized male is a far cry from where he started out—in a loincloth, holding a club. He's evolved from Neanderthalism to cannibalism to Talibanism to hedonism to "what he is today"-ism.

Clinically speaking, testosterone plays a role in both sexes, but the levels in women equal only approximately one-seventh of what is in men. It is produced in their ovaries and adrenal glands and helps maintain muscle and bone strength.

Similar to men, T contributes to sex drive, but after women experience menopause or ovary removal, testosterone production drops off drastically. But if you inject larger than normal amounts of Mr. T into a healthy reproducing female, she tends to have so many sexual thoughts that it literally drives her crazy. (Make a note: Gotta check the levels of T in nymphomaniacs.) Enough said about that for now. Let's get back to men.

This hormone is not only about killing and having sex. Universal medical journals agree ole Testy is key to developing creativity, intellect, thought patterns, assertiveness, and drive, as well as the ability to propose new ideas and carry them through to successful conclusions. Adequate levels of testosterone throughout a man's lifetime helps him to thrive as a child, develop stronger muscles and bones (along with acne) during puberty, cope with stress during peak career years, and age gracefully after retirement.

Has he become complacent and whipped, afraid to say what's on his mind? Is he fearful to do things that were historically earmarked for men only? Has he become a mere shadow of his former generations?

I'm going to say right up front that this is not a medical book or spiritual assessment. We're not going to be doing any clinical studies, and you won't find many footnotes quoted from any journals.

> HAS HE BECOME COMPLACENT AND WHIPPED, AFRAID TO SAY WHAT'S ON HIS MIND?

Au contraire. What follows is a perspective of how most male baby boomers and their offspring are growing up and managing ole Testy, specifically in present-day North America. And if we, as men, have become "less male" in the masculine category, then I guess that's progress. We can only blame or congratulate ourselves depending on how we define progress.

We should, of course, acknowledge that over the last few decades, we've cemented this current foundation with words and actions. And for the most part, I don't know about you, but I can assure you there's a big struggle going on inside me and most men as we desperately search for some kind of *balance* (sexually, socially, corporately) in our new *"equality at all costs"* world.

We, as men (this is the collective "we" as in predominantly North American), are proud to say we are a civilized and an equal opportunity society, right? But has this progression buffered our levels of testosterone? Has our signatory hormone and unique status become an endangered species? Has the ascent of women and their ideals put our most identifiable traits at risk?

You see, men are drawn to those old movies of the samurai, *Gunfight at the O.K. Corral*, or *Run Silent, Run Deep* that pit man against man and show honorable death. And then there's the last scene of *The Good, the Bad and the Ugly* where men are faced with basic survival. Gone are also the days that if you spit in my face, I'll punch your lights out. It's pretty much the opposite now that we have entered into a world of sexual equality. We must maintain self-control at all costs. When I'm with men, I can talk in "man language," but as soon as a woman enters the fray, I must adjust my words to a gentler state of grace or be subjected to judgment. "Alas, poor Yorick! I knew him," to quote Shakespeare's *Hamlet*.

***

I'd like to point out one inequality that will be around longer than time—physical sports. It's true that women can compete at a very high level in athletics. The very best women can beat up on a lot of so-so men, but the crème de la crème, the highest paid, the most physically demanding, the most watched sports all belong to men. And ladies, please don't take this personal. It is just a matter of truth.

Consider boxing, football, basketball, hockey, baseball, soccer, track and field, tennis, golf, even beach volleyball. In fact, men dominate in every professional sport out there where money is the reward. Prize money in tennis may be on a par, but head-to-head, man to woman, there is no comparison. The best men will win every single time. That goes for individual sports and team sports (except maybe some gymnastic events and synchronized swimming where flexibility and holding your breath are key components).

I can see all the feminists getting riled up over this. They're going to say, "Well, what do you expect? Men are built for athletics and competitiveness. How stupid can you be? They're bigger, taller, stronger, and faster by genetic makeup. Of course they're going to beat up on our sisters."

To that reasoning, I must concede. I accept the logic that men are bigger and faster, and so on. So is it a moot point? Let's dig a little deeper. Let's examine competition where physical strength, height, and weight don't matter.

Who's better at darts? How about snooker? Bowling? Maybe Indy cars, dragsters, or horse jockeying? And how about the granddaddy of them all, poker, bridge, or chess? Women compete in these more cerebral contests and appear on some top lists, but rarely break into the ranks of the elite. Perhaps logic is akin to competition in general, and emotion hinders performance. Just throwing it out there. Maybe that's the intrinsic reason why men are tactically better at war.

Again, feminists will wave a dismissive finger, saying, "What's so important about these competitions anyway? Without men, wars and games might not exist. Are they relevant?" They will give evidence of well-established women with positions of power and point out how well they do head-to-head with men. And they're right again.

> WITHOUT MEN, WARS AND GAMES MIGHT NOT EXIST. ARE THEY RELEVANT?

The world tends to operate, at least in many ways, through competition and strategizing. So as a side effect of business, do men have the upper hand because of their high rankings in life games? We have to examine the statistics that reveal which gender starts more businesses versus which one has the better batting average for success. I'll let you guys, both men and women, do the research on this subject and publish the results on your blogs. How does that sound? Let's see who wins that argument. It's not a competition; I only want you guys to lay out the facts so we can all benefit.

The fact is that no matter how politically and sexually equal we'd like to be, there are differences and glaring disparities. Just like men will never win at birthing children, at least not anytime soon. However, this imbalance has not stopped our society from trying to create an equal playing field. We are hell bent on equality in the home and in the office, at work and at play. Make a note that men are, for the most part, in favor of equality. They are also very much aware that it is a great ideal. Note, too, that men have worked side by side with women politically and socially, in spite of their demise, to make it so.

Over the last few decades, men have gracefully learned how to turn the other cheek, admit their weaknesses, and become significantly softer. We even cry in public … and at the movies occasionally (never a pretty sight). In essence we have stopped ourselves from doing what we do best: kill (enemies and food), rape, pillage, protect, and have a lot of sex (not in that order of course). I think most of our generation would rank them in the reverse. These days I don't need to kill my food, but I admit that sometimes I entertain the thought of taking out a few idiots.

Naturally, I'd be a lot happier if I was having a reasonable amount of sex while protecting my family. The pillage, rape, and kill tendencies have drastically decreased, so there's no need to go there unless a crime is committed. Speaking of criminals, a solely male population in a guarded environment may reveal what all men are like if left to their own devices. However, that's a completely different discussion. For the topic at hand, we'll stick with the mainstream population.

It doesn't take much effort to see how drastically we've adapted in a mere two thousand or so years, never mind going back to the origins of mankind. Back when Jesus, Buddha, and Mohammed laid the underpinnings of their religions, our hero was a simpler man. Each new development pushed him to reevaluate and modify his role.

Now, here we are chugging along in time. What is our new purpose? Is it to amass great wealth? Lead people into battle? Become the subservient gender? Are we supposed to find a soul mate or fulfill some predetermined task that was agreed upon before life entered our body? No one has the answer, because if they did I am sure it would be published all over the internet. So which of the above is the correct answer? Where do testosterone and balance fit into the equation? Let's break it down a bit more.

The men in this book currently lurks in the Northern Hemisphere between the Pacific and Atlantic Oceans. Eastern man hangs out geographically from south-east of the Caspian Sea (around Turkey) and encompasses all Asian countries, a significant part of the Middle East, and most of Eastern Europe. Men from *South America, Western Europe, the UK, Central America, Africa, New Zealand, and Australia* don't count because they are not as influenced by our culture.

In our North American cities and towns, our homeboy has been evolving in a place where his basic and most innate instincts have been altered, if you will, by the melting pot forces of the industrial, sexual, racial, and social revolutions within our continent.

In ever-increasing frequency, especially since the 1960s, our hero has been systematically stripped of and made to control his instinctual behaviors in order to exist in peace and harmony. These behaviors include greed, lust, power, and more. He has had to search diligently to find ways to meet the expectations of his family, job, and relationships while suppressing his primal urge to lash out, degrade, kill, and conquer. He must also satisfy his craving for sex without offending someone or ending up in court.

> NO MATTER HOW YOU SLICE IT, DICE IT, OR GRATE IT, TRADITIONAL MAN IS UNDERGOING NON-INVASIVE BRAIN SURGERY.

No matter how you slice it, dice it, or grate it, traditional man is undergoing non-invasive brain surgery. The post-op version is yet to be unveiled. What we can be assured of is that past behaviors and assertiveness that identified man in the days of the Wild West will never be allowed again.

Perhaps not a bad thing, but men are certainly headed toward a precariously softer direction. That fact pisses off a lot of men. It forces them to live a kind of Jekyll and Hyde life. They adopt one persona around like-minded males and another when in mixed company or on the job.

Let's backtrack a tad. Men need testosterone, the "King of hormones," for pretty much every task they perform on a daily basis. Impulses from the brain such as hunt, kill, and conquer, and various sexual thoughts, cause their bodies to create it in abundance. The group of hormones that create and support masculinity is known as androgens, but testosterone is the king. It is the hormone that is primarily responsible for forming otherwise neutral personalities into poets, athletes, gladiators, and aggressive beings.

Testosterone also regulates sex drive and maintains the development of male sexual characteristics, including dominance, emotional and physical strength, body shape, hair growth, and deep voice. All of these things are our birthright. Every man feels the need to dominate and control by physical and emotional strength. He's larger and hairier, and if he can't use a club, knife, or gun, he pounds his opponent into submission with sarcasm and wit.

Now, men behave differently in mixed crowds—they end up in arguments on the job and at home—because we are starting to be at odds with our genes. Men have an enormous balancing act to deal with from playing touch football (we'd rather play tackle 'cause we're so damn competitive) with our kids to running up our credit cards (most toys at the end wins). Even the rules of sexual harassment come into play.

It all boils down to this. With all the testosterone raging through a man's system for the majority of his life, how does he juggle relationships, work, and play without offending someone? How does he control his desires? How in the hell does anyone expect him to keep going forward, with any semblance of balance, when his primal urges are being squashed by social pressure? It's a powder keg waiting for the spark that will set it off.

I ask you, don't men deserve to have fulfilled lives? Simply put, man must control the influence testosterone has on his behavior. He must control his emotional, sexual and, social impulses in order to make it through life without being branded a Neanderthal, or worse. Mr. T, you see, creates a problem. T is built for action. Even the TV show *The A-Team* had a Mr. T to get things done via brute force. His name was no accident.

We all can agree on at least one thing. Things are pretty topsy-turvy in our society these days. From the office to the playground, men have to watch what they say and do. As women ascend in power and influence, men are getting the short end of the stick.

It's a tough grind for today's man. He's had to abandon his traditional role of macho, barbarian gunslinger and become a compassionate, kinder, and giving being. Doesn't that describe Clark Kent, aka Superman? He's able to kick the crap out of criminals as the superhero, and then go back to his day job as a compassionate, mild-mannered reporter for *The Daily Planet.*

If bullets bounced off all men, and we could take out our hostilities without reproach, we too might be able to be gentle and "Clark-like" in our downtime. But that's not how things are in the real world. Kryptonite, in the form of judgment, is everywhere we go.

Is it surprising that the Super Bowl is the most revered and watched sporting event by men in our society? The game awakens every Y chromosome out there. Where else can the viewer feel the adrenalin rush of true warriors in full armor legally trying to hurt each other? I mean, football is war without weapons, right? Its team against team, man against man, and only the, toughest, fastest, and smartest wins the trophy.

No women to judge us here (except the game interviewers on the field and in the locker room). The ones allowed on the sidelines can have opinions, but they're not out on the field competing. Then there's the curvy, sexy ones with pom-poms on the sidelines. It's straight out of the Middle Ages. Men in armor waging war while women cheer them on. What could be more natural and satisfying?

I would bet a dump truck full of cash that during football games, while a man is sipping beer and chomping on a hot dog dripping in mustard and fried onions, he is actually pretty damn happy. He probably feels balanced too. The packed arenas, live streaming sites, and even online betting all validate this fact. In that environment man feels good about himself. He's there to witness the conflict, the action, and the blood. He's there for the cheering, drinking, swearing, eating, and being obnoxious. These rituals bond him to others like him. That's why he is willing to pay a lot of money to attend.

Think of Sherwood Forest and Robin Hood's band of merry men. They eat with their hands while carving flesh off a roasted pig while their women nestle up for warmth. There's horseplay and laughter all around. Life is simple, and everyone works together for the betterment of all. But when Prince John and his goons show up, Robin's boys jump into the fray in a heartbeat.

That is the essence of a man. There's not one second of hesitation when we're up against oppression. We love action. We love to defend our homes and our women. That's because all rational men understand eating, fighting, and the love of a woman. Of course, these kinds of conflicts are virtually nonexistent in today's society, but it doesn't alter the fact that men are drawn to territorial violence, something to which women are not so inclined.

> MEN NEED TIME TO BE WITH OTHER MEN IN A PRIMAL ENVIRONMENT SO THEY CAN RELEASE TENSIONS THAT FEMALES DON'T HAVE.

Men need time to be with other men in a primal environment so they can release tensions that females don't have. This is why our hero mingles in sports bars, golf courses, pool halls, strip clubs, and locker rooms. This is why he loves WWE and UFC fights.

He yearns to be free, uninhibited, and to feel the warrior presence. He can't do that in the presence of women. He can't do that in a politically correct environment. He can't do that at a dance social. He can't do that at the office party. He can't do that when he's surrounded by his mixed bowling team. He can't even do that in marriage.

This is precisely why he goes hunting, fishing, or camping with his buddies for the weekend in the middle of nowhere. He needs to be left alone. He yearns to escape the political correctness he faces in every other area of his life.

Those kinds of sanctuaries are the last bastions where he can swear, spit, and tell uncensored jokes. In short, he can be himself and doesn't have to worry about being judged.

In these all-male get-togethers, he can let loose for a while, so that when he returns to the world of "equality," he can justify his submission to his day-to-day reality. He is forced to survive in a world of deception and denial. But must he stay there forever? Can he find happiness, love, and balance as he walks on egg shells through the years?

In the following chapters, I will take you on a journey as we look at the various stages of our hero's growth and maturity. We will observe how our hero searches for, and potentially finds, *testosteronic balance* in the twenty-first century. At the end of each chapter, the forlorn lad receives a grade of how he's doing physically and mentally.

I hope you find the progression enlightening and can identify with specific periods of his life. Hopefully, you will learn the secrets of how to achieve balance and be happy. After all, the purpose of this book is to help you be all that you can be, despite having to struggle within our North American world of confusion and chaos.

CHAPTER 4

THE STRUGGLE BEGINS: LITTLE BOYS UNDER FIVE

I admit that I don't recall much from my childhood, so I had to think of a way to go back in time and remember what it was like being a little boy. However, all that is necessary is to observe any parent with a male child under five years of age. It doesn't take long to see that most young boys are out of balance even without an excess of testosterone in their system.

To confirm my hunch, I visited the waiting room at a pediatric office. I observed mothers, and a couple of fathers who had taken on the role of mother, getting their little tykes prepped for an appointment with the doctor. Most of the kids were healthy and just there for a checkup. At any given time, there were at least a dozen rambunctious kids scattered around the room.

The drill ran true for 99 percent of all I surveyed. Nearly every parent gave their child instructions on how to behave, but for every positive word they spoke, there were a dozen that went the other way.

"Don't put that dirty book in your mouth."

"Don't touch that toy. It has germs."

"Leave that magazine alone. You can't have it."

"Share that toy. That's his ball. Give it back."

"Don't push that little girl."

A myriad of do's and don'ts were flying around the waiting room at breakneck speed. My head was snapping back and forth, like I was watching a heated match at Wimbledon. Yet, for all the negativity thrust upon those tiny tots, the temper tantrums were relatively few. The children who did throw a tantrum received stern looks from the parents of the "well-behaved" children. That usually led to the offender being snatched up and given either a harsh berating or the silent stare treatment until tears flowed. Magically, a few moments later, the boy child was back in the thick of things and mingling with what initiated the behavior in the first place.

So it went, one by one, as I watched parents and their offspring come and go. Two hours flew by, and I left with my notes. Here are my findings: Boys tended to be more inquisitive, louder, and more aggressive than the little girls. Boys made more noise and objected more to being controlled than little girls. Boys tended to be more selfish with the available toys. In general, the boys were harder to deal with whether the parent was male or female.

***

When you think about it, it is a minor miracle that children, especially boys, arrive at kindergarten with so few hang-ups. When you retrace your early parenting days, all you can remember, besides the dimpled smiles and laughter, is the multitude of times you stopped your child from licking the floor or prevented him from falling down a flight of stairs.

Of course, whose little boy hasn't licked the floor ... or worse? What little boy hasn't burnt his fingers, fallen down stairs, or wrecked a bicycle? I mean, that's how the boy child learns, right? By getting into trouble or getting injured.

Basically, we endeavor to mold the little tykes into to a level of "normal" within the confines of our own family's parameters. We hold the lads back, either by stern words or looks, and discourage any further exploration into a particular part of the kitchen cupboard, closet, drawer, or sand-box.

Some parents take the more traditional approach of slapping their child's hands or bottom, though these methods seem to no longer be mainstream.

Another approach is the dreaded "time out." That's where the little bugger gets a chance to reflect on what he's done wrong, as if he really cares. He waits his mandatory two minutes, and everything magically returns to hunky-dory. There is no remnant of fear for what he's done wrong, so when he does it again, the stunned parent can't understand why.

What this teaches the little boy is that if he waits a few minutes, the one in charge will forgive what happened, or if he simply apologizes, all is forgiven. What a great lesson, right? How easy it is to please the weary parent, who thinks his little rascal is so cute.

Later in life, he tries the same tactic at work or with his

buddies. He's perplexed that he can't placate the opposition as easily. In fact, he's usually branded a selfish jerk for that kind of behavior. Does this truly surprise anyone? Of course, little girls can be equally selfish in their behavior, and maybe this because in many ways young children are just beginning to develop and there's not that much testosterone influence yet, so let's explore further.

It's funny, in a way, how a good swat from my parents always got the job done when I was young. Fear and pain got the point across fast, but I guess we've become more tolerant. In our more modern world, we don't want our kids to suffer. God forbid. The number of emotional disorders that have sprung up in the past several years is astounding: ADHD, ODD, ASD, Bipolar, and the list goes on. None of these existed when I was growing up. We were just kids. I guess parenting has come down to loving your kids to death and hoping for the best.

Perhaps one reason for the kinder, more forgiving style of parenting is due to the dual-income family, which limits quality time parents get to spend with their kids. Is this why we try to take the nonviolent approach, or is this the definition of a higher form of civilization? Of course, violence in our society is being suppressed, and we can all agree that's a good thing.

But otherwise, this "on our home turf" nonaggression mentality is incredible. Especially when you consider that, overseas, our armed forces and various extremist groups are busy blowing each other up. Does that mean their values are ahead … or behind the curve?

***

Let's go back to the idea of your little boy's balance and the amount of hormones he has at a tender young age. When you add up the number of times you hold him back, granted mostly for his own protection, you wonder how he stays inquisitive. We are amazed at how the tiny lad continually pushes for and wants to try new things. This is due in part to his testosterone levels, as well as a natural instinct for learning. Surely most parents wholeheartedly encourage this kind of inquisitiveness, and they are proud of their son's growth until the poor kid enters school.

Few parents are surprised when one of the first questions they are compelled to ask their little boy when he returns from a few days of school is, "Who taught you that?" As a parent, you scratch your head wondering if every mannerism or morale values you've meticulously engrained into his head is going to be replaced by the dogma of peer pressure.

Yikes! You've spent so much time trying to tattoo those values into your kid's psyche, and now those other parents' cretons are bent on destroying all the work you've put into your gifted little boy.

The scorecard on whether or not he will be positively or negatively affected draws a non-conclusive grade at this point. Perhaps it's in line with the hormonal thing, because he's still too young to have a significant amount of testosterone surging through his body. We'll find out later what the true effects of peer pressure will be on our hero.

This is life for the boy under five years of age. He's busy learning how to walk, talk, and use a toilet, as well as show off his newly learned mannerisms on the behalf of his parents. The poor boy's words and behaviors are definitely skewed by the time he hits school. He struggles through his newfound freedom and lessons trying to please everyone. He's a little messed up, but time is on his side.

Scoreboard: *After the first five years*

Testosterone: Levels are relatively low and there is no real influence

Balance: Too much chaos and too much to mentally digest. Ignorance is bliss.

Score for this chapter: Out of balance

Total: Out of balance: 1   In balance: 0

WARNING! Chapters 5–7 are graphic due to testosterone hitting its full stride and may offend younger readers. Even older readers who've been through it may find these descriptions and situations uncomfortable. Try to keep an open mind!

CHAPTER 5

PRECARIOUS PRETEENS AND TEENS

Puberty. Need one say anything more? The first serious infusion of testosterone. Of course the kid is out of balance. Other boys are growing faster, or slower, than him. Some kids even have facial and body hair.

Young men often begin noticing their physical differences during gym classes. Some schools have group showers, and this can be a traumatic experience for a young man. Boys get a whole new perspective on self-identity when they see what other semi-naked guys have "down there." Talk about insecurity. Jeez! In addition to all of that, this is a time that young men begin taking notice of girls and dealing with the unfamiliar affects hormones have on their mind and body. These things take a boy way out of balance!

This point in a young man's life is spent trying to figure out if he's any good at anything. He hears how being involved in sports can make parents proud, and more importantly, is attractive to girls. On the other hand, getting good grades, singing in the school choir, or joining the math club is up for grabs. Trying to decide what to do and wondering if he'll be viewed as manly or a wimp. It's like walking a tightrope, and with teenage hormones working overtime, it's a challenging situation at best. It's a precarious time, with no clear answers.

Your voice is just about to change, but your father is already calling you a young man. What the heck does that mean? At twelve years old, you still like Captain Crunch and watching cartoons. You're also learning that there are things you like to do that others don't and vice versa. So you keep somethings to yourself, so you won't be judged. You're learning discretion.

Then there's the preteen, middle school dances. You know the deal. The girls on one side, doing the step-ball-change move in their miniskirts, while the guys are on the other side laughing at each other. Then suddenly, you notice one of your more mature classmates hitting on the girl you've had your eye on. Ouch! Your first taste of jealousy, which combined with your current amount of new hormones, creates a serious state of imbalance.

You try not to watch, but you can't stop thinking about him wrapping his arms around your crush. Secretly, you can't help but wonder how that feels. When the dance is over, she smiles at you, but instead of stepping up to the plate, you turn away and tell your buddies that dancing is for pansies. However, your inner voice is calling you a wimp.

That same inner voice begins to speak up more frequently. It can prompt you to act in certain ways. At this time in your life, it's a little mysterious and easy to miss. Is the voice related to the new hormones your body is now producing? Is it the testosterone speaking? Not sure? So let's see if that comes into play later and get back to the issue at hand.

Maybe you muster up the strength to walk over and ask the girl for the next slow dance, and she accepts. Hot damn, this pansy stuff has its rewards. You hold sweaty hands, but you're even more embarrassed about your bodies touching as you dance. Naturally, such close proximity to a girl you find attractive produces certain feelings—physical feelings you are not accustomed to having at this point in your life.

You get the message from your brain, but its all uncertainty at this point. In other words, you don't really know what to do with those sensations, or if you are supposed to do anything at all. Later on, of course, you begin to figure things out.

Back to the school dance. Neither you nor your crush have the faintest idea how to move to the music. There you are, in a semi-clutch, holding hands, stiff-legged and swaying at the waist. You don't understand why your palms are sweaty, your heart is racing, your cheeks are flushed, and your throat is dry. And it's still there after the dance is over as you walk back across the floor.

By the time you reach your friends, they're all laughing at you. Testosterone's influence makes you take a fake swat at a couple of them. You push each other around, and then things quiet down. Except you can't get that girl out of your mind. What's more, that feeling lingers for days. What's up with that?

You go home thinking about why being that close to a girl made such an impact. Then one day in science class, your teacher introduces the topic of hormones. You find out about the effects that testosterone has on your body, and

> YOU GO HOME THINKING ABOUT WHY BEING THAT CLOSE TO A GIRL MADE SUCH AN IMPACT.

things begin to make sense. What a revelation! The feelings you experienced at the dance is a WOW factor! Suddenly, you begin to develop a fondness for science class and look forward to learning more about the male and female body.

Invariably, most every young man becomes exposed to *Playboy, Penthouse*, or some other porno magazine. Those provocative full-color, high-quality nude photographs contrast sharply with the generic bland black-and-white photos from science class that create a source of blood flow that has only recently started to mean something. From that moment on, testosterone moves into your bloodstream and you can't stop thinking about girls. It becomes a major distraction.

Around this same time, girls are figuring out some things too. They're dealing with hormones of their own, and their bodies undergo significant changes. They notice that boys begin to pay more attention to them, and the more they develop, the more intense that attention becomes. The more they try to look attractive, the more Mr. T wreaks havoc on the young male.

However, boys are too immature, or should I say uninformed, to realize what is really going on inside their bodies. But at this point they don't care. The man-child wants to get as much info as he can about girls. He wants to know what makes them attracted to a boy. Science class is of no help here. Everything they teach about sex sounds so clinical and formal. The teacher mentions "intercourse," and you wonder of that's the same thing as making love, or is it different? You wonder if any of your classmates know more than you do, or even have experience? Too many questions and not enough answers.

Becoming a full teenager creeps up on you. The testosterone ramps up too. You get hair on your arms and in your armpits. Your voice drops an octave. You think you feel some stubble on your upper lip. You feel stronger, and your muscles become more defined. If you flex hard enough, you can actually see some definition forming on your calf. It's absolutely not as defined as your upper quads, but it's starting to look solid. The biceps are feeling it too.

However, some of the most powerful changes are of a sexual nature. Testosterone production is high, and this has multiple effects on a young man's mind and body. Yes, there are erections, both expected and unexpected. Thoughts are often dominated by a desire for sex or sexual release. All of this happens on a regular basis, and it's almost an annoyance because there is no escaping it.

You hear about orgasms in class, but you have no real understanding of any of it. No one offers any real, definitive explanations. You also hear or read about masturbation. At some point, you may even experiment with it. Certainly, everyone from your parents to religious leaders strongly discourage it. However, testosterone has no morals and no mercy, and at some point, you give in and begin the up and down movements that give you pulsating pleasure that ends up with ejaculation.

> HOWEVER, TESTOSTERONE HAS NO MORALS AND NO MERCY.

Whether orgasm is self-inflicted or brought about by another, the influence of testosterone has entered a new phase. This sends our hero reeling and totally out of balance once again. From this point on, when Mr. T kicks in, it's a direct line and the message is clear. If it's a fight, T goes to the muscles. If it involves arousal, then it goes to the brain and the loins.

Any discussions of additional sexual issues are best left for the next chapter when our young adult gets more experience with the opposite sex. Will our young man move toward a more balanced existence?

Scoreboard: *After the precarious preteen/teen years*

Testosterone: Levels are rising and creating havoc.

Balance: Too much chaos and too much to mentally digest

Score for this chapter: Out of balance

Total: Out of balance: 2   In balance: 0

CHAPTER 6

BOY BECOMES MAN

Watch out world, testosterone is in full circulation and poised to kick butt. Once a boy approaches twenty, in his mind he's a man. By that time, he knows just about everything there is to know about everything. They've gone through their teenage years, totally misunderstood, and completely opposed to pretty much everything their parents stood for. In fact, he's pretty much opposed to everything everyone stands for, but he has great friends. They hang out together, drinking beer and partying. It's all part of the process of becoming a responsible man.

But where are we with testosterone and balance? Well, as it turns out, men must churn through an adolescent learning curve before they can compute the effects those events will have on Mr. T.

By trial and error, the man-child finds out for himself about the next level of do's and don'ts. That takes some initiative, because he's drinking, partying, and maybe even experimenting with drugs. Instinctively, he knows it's all wrong, but he's gotta do what he's gotta do to be part of the "in crowd."

But there are much bigger fish to fry as a high schooler armed with Mr. T. Life throws out a variety of temptations, and you're eager to get a taste. You have to decide whether or not to smoke, do drugs, get laid, be the strong silent type, or just a nice guy.

You need to establish your wardrobe and image. You can be trendy or run around in ripped jeans and muscle tees. Of course, a lot of this is driven by your finances, your physique, and the amount of T surging through your body.

You can swear a lot, spit a lot, steal, and be arrogant, or you can be polite and respectful. (Remember the morality your parents tried to instill with you before you hit grade school? "Peer pressure" can be overpowering here.)

Let's face it; the boorish scenario is what comes naturally. However, your part-time job requires you to be polite and respectful or you won't get money to impress the chicks. It's one of the first balancing acts you master. So it seems, you're capable of multiple personalities depending on who you're with. All affect T in different ways.

When you're at school, with your friends and in the comfort zone, you are what they expect you to be. This may be the closest to who you actually are. But when you're at home, you are what your parents expect you to be. When you're at your part-time job, you're in that mode and so on and so on. It's takes time to sort out the real you. God forbid, people think you're a wimp.

So you try to approach the world with a manly attitude, and sometimes that leads to fighting. It seems as though every boy gets into a fight at this age, no matter if he's the class bully or a baby-faced nerd. It also seems that most every guy gets his ass kicked too, often more than once. I don't mean a slap in the face or a few pushes.

Most of the time a fight starts out with a playful push at a party, making eye contact with the wrong guy, or flirting with someone else's girl. Next thing you know, a fight erupts.

It can happen in the schoolyard, gym, back alley, or right in front of your house. It can be one on one, or five against one. You go home bloodied and bruised. When it happens, the fear of it happening again can last a lifetime, and it is one of the many reasons our society doesn't condone it. We prefer nonviolent, diplomatic solutions. Nevertheless, due directly to Mr. T, violence persists.

We are encouraged not to lash out. To save face, we substitute physical violence with sarcasm or just flip of "a bird" to piss someone off. Neither is very satisfying for a man. They only build up rage, because it suppresses Mr. T which may result in a surplus of anxiety and anger. This is why some guys seem to just snap out of the blue.

Getting back to the aftermath of a fight. You return home a little worse for wear. Your parents want to know who beat you up. Sometimes you know, sometimes you don't. Sometimes you tell, sometimes you can't. As you approach manhood, you realize your parents won't always be there to protect you, and you'll have to face that crowd on your own. So you try to take your wounds in stride, and be stronger for it. You try to prepare for the next potential confrontation and use your brain.

Surely, that's why the first caveman grabbed a club. If he wasn't strong enough to win, then he needed an advantage. He used his brain and pounded the crap out of his enemy. In the aftermath, he felt superior and kept that club near his side. Little did he know that the Cro-Magnon he beat up was working on a longer and sharper spear. Later came knives, then guns, and the rest is history.

Physically fighting another person is another thing that most girls never experience. You see, since the beginning of time, the male species has been set up to fight. Whether it be for food, territory, possessions, or his woman. Thus the need for a hormone like testosterone.

When the village was ransacked, the women and children were usually stashed away. The community would live or die by the strength of the male population. Few women will know the pleasure of physical destruction, and believe me, when men fight, they prefer to finish their enemy right on the spot. There is a primal pleasure in conquering. Just look at famous boxing great like Muhammed Ali, Mike Tyson, Sugar Ray Leonard and Floyd Mayweather or UFC champs like Georges St. Pierre, Jon Jones and Anderson Silva. These are iconic men in violent sports that have transcended the general population and are adorned by millions.

> YOUNG BOYS MUST FLEX THEIR MUSCLES AS THEY GROW. IT IS PRIMAL LAW.

Competition between men—and the need to know who is stronger and who can survive in combat—is what adrenalin and testosterone were made for.

Brothers and best friends go through this all the time while growing up. It's not uncommon for the odd elbow smash or errant foot in the face to come from nowhere. Often, fooling around results in a bloody nose or a broken tooth. That said, it's probably the most normal form of bonding and display of T between maturing males. Young boys must flex their muscles as they grow. It is primal law. If we got marooned on an island, our strength and brainpower would be our only tools for survival. Just because we've invented and evolved in society doesn't change what's inside of us. We were created to survive. Take us out of our comfortable homes and cities, and we'd soon revert to the basics. Believe me, testosterone would be welcomed in a hostile world.

***

Fight or flight. We've all heard about it, but when you're a boy and the playful pushing and shoving starts, it doesn't take long for the real punches to follow. Powerful punches, the kind that can knock you down. Painful punches that smash and rearrange your face. Make no mistake, when the fight starts the goal, regardless of geographical location, is always total domination.

Take most any man, place him anywhere on the planet in a hand-to-hand combat situation, and he will not stop until either himself or his opponent cannot move. The reasoning behind that kind of brutality is simple. To render your opponent harmless and unable to ever come after you again. Viva testosterone!

I think, intrinsically, Eastern and Western men have no differences here. But a young Western man (boy) is definitely taught to hold back, to discourage physical fighting, and to negotiate. It's difficult because it goes against the genes and DNA of the male organism. But at home and in the streets, we are working hard to promote this as a higher form of civilization. And we are winning. Of course, women are applauding this less barbaric approach to society and why not? It is the more civilized way.

Some say this move toward passivity makes us better

humans, and it does. However, the truth is that this form of less aggression is viewed as weakness in some societies and it can open the door to manipulation. I guess it depends whether you were trained as a marine, mercenary, IT person, or maybe a doctor. It depends on your possessions, income, neighborhood, and your reason to live. The lifestyle we choose is directly related to how we might react to aggression. The end result of our chosen profession puts limits on our hero's ability to let himself express his T and balance.

Let's get back to when our young hero got his ass whooped. The threat and fear that someone out there is trying to do him harm can cause him to face each day with trepidation. There is no greater deterrent or motivation than fear, and that includes greed. You see, in large part Eastern man does not have the same values or concerns. His testosterone levels are unchecked. He looks down on his women, fights, or even kills at will. Fair play is not a part of his makeup. Only survival.

Guns, natural disasters, disease, rape, and death have surrounded him most of his life, and material possessions are few and far between. It's kill or be killed, and T is at the top of the heap for this kind of existence.

A wise man once said, "If you want to stop violence, poverty, and death in poor countries, then educate and give everyone material wealth so that family life will have meaning. If we did that, every man would have something to lose if he became violent. Give people houses, gardens, cars, and luxury instead of guns, and there'd be no need for guns." Of course, this is a pipe dream in Third and Fourth World countries which pulls against the grain of opportunistic capitalists, of which abound in our free society. This is another form of testosteronic competition that we could write a whole other book about, so let's not go there.

Let's focus on our homegrown men, who must take into consideration material wealth, social status, political and sexual correctness into every decision they make. There must be balance or they can lose it all. These amenities make our guys more complicated, putting a restriction on how far testosterone can drive them. It's a constant tug of war between their intellect and their physicality. We'll develop this further as we go through the later stages of our hero's life.

***

Another decision to make during this season of life is how deeply to involve oneself in booze and drugs. It's certainly our right to do illicit stimuli now and then if we so choose. Our parents probably abused everything that was available to them, and the majority seem to have turned out okay.

Socially, you go with the flow. At least for a while anyway. Sooner or later you wake up one day swearing to stop, or at least draw the line on how much you drink, smoke, or snort. This is good because it forces you to have power over those substances. You may slip from time to time, but overall you get it under control. Naturally, you hide all of this from your parents, or tell them half-truths.

***

High school is when you really begin finding out more about the opposite sex. Most girls are well developed by this time, and Mr. T forces you to pay attention.

When I think back on high school, I flashback to room 204, my homeroom for my sophomore year. I remember being half asleep with my head on the desk, waiting for roll call. Suddenly, from out of the blue, came an intoxicating

HIGH SCHOOL IS WHEN YOU REALLY BEGIN FINDING OUT MORE ABOUT THE OPPOSITE SEX. scent that penetrated my nasal passages and went straight to my brain. French, I believe, and expensive without a doubt.

The wonderful scent emanated from a beautiful brunette who glided past me on her way to her seat. She wore a tight angora sweater and plaid miniskirt. The outfit, combined with the heavenly scent, quickly got my attention.

My mind came out of hibernation and my eyes snapped open. My head swiveled with nostrils flared as I followed the semi-blurred image. The perfume made her even more alluring. It was sweet torture.

This mystery of the opposite sex ramps up testosterone production and drags the male teenager out of balance, mostly because answers are not within his grasp. Why should it be any other way? Isn't that why we're physically and mentally opposite? Wouldn't it be amazing if women actually helped us find balance because of these differences?

Other high school balance and "testy" problems revolve around being part of a clique or gang. It's tough to know whether you should be hangin' with the rough and tough athletes who go out every weekend and wreak havoc on people's homes … or park in the library and read National Geographic. Football players are mostly badasses with lots of blatant displays of Mr. T. They try to seduce all the girls and pretty much demolish things just for fun.

I remember going through a parking lot with these goons. They were practicing their forearm shivers on side-view mirrors of docile autos as they walked between the rows. I had to stop one of my linemen so he wouldn't knock the mirror off my car too. I almost got into a fight, until my half-drunken backfield partner told the meathead we were on the same team.

***

Another blatant example pushing testosterone to full throttle is when bad girls encourage and are attracted to bad boys. They always have been, and they always will be. It's human nature. For instance, the swashbuckling devil-may-care kind of guy is extremely desirable and shows up in a lot of movies. Naturally, the testosterone is overflowing from his every pore. For us older people we'd think of actors like Sean Connery, Charles Bronson, Kirk Douglas, John Wayne, Tony Curtis, Yul Brenner, and Burt Lancaster. Younger folks would instantly think of guys like Matt Damon, Denzel Washington, George Clooney, Brad Pitt, Will Smith, Clive Owen, Wesley Snipes, Jackie Chan, and Tom Cruise. All influential role models and all of them saturated with good old T. These bombastic throw downs always get the hot seductive chicks. That leads to either sex or dumping her in the next scene.

We are drawn to these men for their ability to alternate from being bad boys to intelligent thinkers, as well as their ability to show emotion and compassion. In movies, the ability to balance testosterone has been written into the script. No one worries about, or has to deal with, the consequences.

However, decade after decade and movie after movie, this brutal machoism never seems to stop femme fatales from going after the super-empowered, over-emasculated stud. Men get it. Men like those results. In fact, we love those scenes and certainly try to emulate similar behaviors in our search for success, beautiful babes, and sex. Can you blame us for this stereotyping? In real life, women slap you in the face, or dump you like a drunken sailor, when you behave that foolish. We have to remember that these encounters only happen on film. On our way out of the theatre, we reset our minds for reality.

Of course, not all guys play football or are rough and tumble. There's the egghead, the math geek, or the choir boy. They, too, wonder about the girls, but let's face it, we're talking about another division of the food chain.

The guys that don't play sports, drive motorcycles, or possess copious amounts of cash are typically relegated to the plain Janes. These tend to be nice girls who don't cause any trouble—the ones the bad asses would be happy to introduce to their parents in a few years. But for now, they're still too sweet.

> ALL YOUNG MEN STRUGGLE TO FIND THEIR COMFORT ZONE AND THEIR RUNG ON THE LADDER OF LOVE.

All young men struggle to find their comfort zone and their rung on the ladder of love. If you're really fortunate and possess athletic ability, good looks, and a voice, then you have a bigger problem. When you're with the athletes, they undermine you because you sing in the choir. However, when you get the lead in the school musical, those same jocks are jealous 'cause all the chicks are hanging on you.

Everyone loves to hate a winner, including the lead girl's boyfriend, who is willing to punch you out because you get to give her that open-mouth kiss day after day in rehearsals. He gets even more infuriated when you inhale her in front of everyone, including him, during matinee and evening performances.

As a matter of fact, as opening night comes and goes, she

starts falling for you via the character you've been living as an actor. A mild victory for Mr. T? A perfect reason why the boyfriend and two of his buddies begin following your car when you and the leading lady are out for a ride.

They chase you all over town for the better part of an hour, leaning on your rear bumper like a squad car looking for a bust until you finally stop at your friend Fritz's house. You'll need backup when the inevitable happens. You ring the doorbell just as the soon-to-be-former boyfriend, Bruno, pulls into the driveway for a face-to-face. Three against one.

Fritz walks out in a white tank top holding a Louisville Slugger. It was enough to hold the other two back while Bruno and you duke it out. He was a guard; you're a halfback and forty pounds lighter. However, being taller and quicker with the reach advantage, you land five or so jabs, then a couple of crosses and uppercuts to his face. That does the trick but leaves you with a broken pinky on your left hand and a broken thumb on your right.

Shit! After an encounter like that, you realize how fake the movies are. Real fighting causes real injuries and long-lasting pain. You drive the forlorn damsel home using the insides of your wrists. The pain lasted a while, but his face was a bruised mess for all to see. The story spreads around school like wildfire. At least it got you kudos with your pals and other girls interested. Testosterone at work? All and all, getting the recognition was worth the broken bones.

Meanwhile, after the fight, your leading lady tells Bruno to take a hike. The victor gets the spoils. It's Samson and Delilah, Anthony and Cleopatra century after century. Strangely enough, the romance died shortly after the school play had its run. The only thing that remained after the breakup was the recalcification in your healing hands.

***

But let's get back to fundamentals. When you're under twenty, you want to hook up with women, wear cool clothes, drive a hot car, have your own private email/Facebook/twitter address, and own a big wide flat-screen TV. This enables you to watch sports, MTV, and all your rentals in HD. Surely, with this kind of entertainment at hand, life comes to you.

But despite having a part-time job, most of the money still flows from the overprotective parent who feels obligated to give you more than they got from their parents. So life is pretty easy. You might not get the Hugo Boss T's that cost a hundred and fifty bucks, but you get most of the brand-name stuff you want.

You're getting fed, housed, and pampered—and you have more freedom than you can handle. Living at home is bliss. The only stress is explaining why you are staying out so late and sleeping in so much.

"Shouldn't you look for a better job?" Your mom or dad mutter one day, but you pretend they were joking and leave in a hurry, hoping the subject would disappear as fast as you just did. Everyone says, "Enjoy your youth. You have the rest of your life to make money." Anyway, you're certain you'll be an executive in a few years, making six figures and delegating to your underlings, so why rush things?

Bottom line, if you take out the garbage, give mom the mandatory kiss on the cheek when you leave for school, score a goal or a touchdown, and keep decent grades, everyone is cool and you get enough money to pay for pretty much what you want.

You might have a girlfriend or maybe not. You may have lost your virginity, or maybe you haven't. At this point in time, it doesn't much matter. What does matter is you're getting ready to go out there, overcome all obstacles, begin your assault on the world, and see where Mr. T takes you.

Day to day, you're good. When you think about it, those late teenage years are usually the high points of one's remembered life. It's because the balance between money, possessions, and lack of responsibility, coupled with your parents' blessings, produces a well-rounded lifestyle.

Even though you may find yourself fighting introductory levels of testosterone, you are pretty much in the sweet spot. Hence, by the time a young man reaches twenty, if he's out of jail, hasn't become a drug addict, alcoholic, knocked someone up, or borrowed money to pay for an abortion, he is fairly balanced.

Scoreboard: *By the time I'm twenty*

Testosterone: On the rise big time and is toying with both our heads, but we're not overwhelmed just yet.

Balance: Take away the fascination of the opposite sex and the boy is in balance.

Score for this chapter: Balance

Total: Out of balance: 2   In balance: 1

CHAPTER 7

SPREADING HIS SEED

Two bulls were at the top of a hill overlooking a dozen cows grazing in the pasture.

The young bull faced the older bull. "Look at those two beauties off to the right. Why don't we run down as fast as we can and have sex with them right now?"

The older bull looked over his shoulder at the herd, and then said calmly, "Why don't we walk down and have sex with them all?"

Some readers may find this chapter offensive; however, most men won't. The things we're about to discuss run true whether our hero seeks higher education or enters the workforce. The only difference is where the parties take place. Dorms and frat houses, or houses and apartments. It doesn't matter.

This chapter highlights further the power and influence testosterone has on a young male. Levels increase and affect nearly every area of his life, whether he likes it or not.

Seduction! Lust! Fondling and sexual encounters with women are thoughts that fill a man's mind with constant images and fantasies. The fact is, biologically speaking a man in his early twenties is on a rampage to have sex with any woman who is willing. He is constantly thinking about ways to make that happen, and he is willing to go to great lengths to ensure it does. Believe me, what drives a man into this sexual frenzy has nothing to with a desire to procreate or adding another limb to the family tree. It's all about the thrill of the chase and conquest.

> THE FACT IS, BIOLOGICALLY SPEAKING A MAN IN HIS EARLY TWENTIES IS ON A RAMPAGE TO HAVE SEX WITH ANY WOMAN WHO IS WILLING.

We've all seen or read about how kings in Europe bedded pretty much any woman they desired, or about sheiks and their harems. It seems obvious that men are built for lust, pure and simple. Sex is the goal, and testosterone is there to make sure it happens.

Every man has seen images depicting Roman orgies where half-naked gladiators lay among a bevy of bare-breasted women who are feeding them grapes, all while having unlimited sex. It's a hallucination in our modern society, and we know that sort of thing is not going to happen, but that doesn't mean the fantasy is not still lurking in the minds of many men.

I'm sure every man remembers well his first sexual encounter with a woman. The heart pounding as his body responds to the wonders of her body. Testosterone led him to that moment, and once there, it will not release its hold until the mission has been accomplished.

Once a man has experienced sex, he immediately wants

> **ONCE A MAN HAS EXPERIENCED SEX, HE IMMEDIATELY WANTS IT AGAIN AND AS OFTEN AS POSSIBLE.**

it again and as often as possible. He makes the decision to pursue sex as a goal and with as many women as he can. His parents probably advised him to wait till marriage, but no way that's going to happen.

The words from the song "Principles of Lust" by the pop band Enigma sum up the male's ongoing search for sex: "*The principals of lust are easy to understand. Do what you feel, feel until the end. The principals of lust are burned within your mind. Do what you want, do it until you find love.*" And "doing it" rises to the top of list.

It's not that we don't want love ... or like girls. In fact, we like them a lot, especially for sex, but for other things too. Men simply need to sow their oats. It's the male mandate. This drive is so strong that many men intentionally set out to bed as many women as possible, with no intention whatsoever of forming a long-lasting relationship. If a man doesn't think in this way, he knows men who do. Thankfully, most grow out of it.

Sex becomes an obsession. The medieval poet John Donne was an expert on describing two lovers in bed and how the sun and moon revolved around them during that rapturous, lustful moment. However, the difference between lusting and loving can be blurred by the influence of testosterone.

When in the throes of passion, it's the only thing you're thinking about. It's a kind of blind bliss, as if you've caught the pass and are running toward the end zone and nothing can stop you. You put points on the board and do the celebratory dance.

This doesn't necessarily stop as we age either. Perhaps balance and control of testosterone's influence dictates that we learn passion and love as we get past the one-night stands, and that's a good thing. In truth, even at this early age, we are looking for love and to be loved. This is a critical point in a male's development: namely, the imperativeness to learn how to make love. This can contribute hugely to the management of the Mr. T puzzle. But alas, at this stage, most men haven't got the necessary experience, patience, or desire to know the true meaning of love. They understand lust, and for now, that's what drives them.

One thing I've never understood is the disparity in sex drives between men and women. Men hit their peak in their late teens, early twenties; women get theirs in late twenties, early thirties. Who decided on this out-of-sync formula? It's a mountain to cross as relationships and families take shape. Another glaring difference in how we're set up.

Sex alone has never been the basis of a long-lasting relationship. Both men and women know this. However, at this age, the testosterone-driven man is not quite at the commitment level of Romeo and Juliet. In fact, he's quite happy to keep all of that for later. Furthermore, as North Americans, we experienced the one and only sexual revolution of the 1960s. This event only added fuel the flame. You see, the birth control pill not only opened the door to casual sex forever, but it gave the woman the upper hand on who she wanted to seduce and caused the first unnatural ripple in the history of testosterone.

So with "the pill" preventing them from becoming pregnant, woman started to take control of their sexual desires, mates, and fates. Even through the 1970s and '80s, when statistically speaking STDs were at all-time lows, a woman's worst fear was becoming pregnant. Therefore, with the dread of pregnancy virtually wiped out, men were at the mercy of willful, wanton women, and until AIDS popped up, sex was rampant throughout the land.

This is important in terms of balance and Mr. T. For up until the pill, men had always done the chasing and worked hard to get laid, even though it was pretty much the woman's call. But the newly liberated female predator was on the lustful prowl with a carefree attitude and doing his work for him. It was a full-blown role reversal, and make no mistake, this really confused men and knocked the scales way out of balance. It put a chink in testosterone's armor.

**

I remember one beautiful girl who picked me up at a bar, took me to her place, and demanded sex. Afterward, she got up, put her robe on, and looked down at me. "That was great. I'm going for a shower," she said. "Could you clean up? I'd appreciate it if you're gone when I come back. I like to sleep alone. Don't worry about the door. It self-locks."

Holy moly! Talk about being devastated. I gathered my things like a mouse retreating to its hole, got dressed, and let myself out. Moments later, I found myself on a strange street, at three in the morning, trying to remember where I left my car. If I have ever made a women feel like that, then shoot me. That humbling experience taught me to be more sensitive in how I treated women after seduction. This was a significant milestone in the balancing of Mr. T. This led to a new

> THIS WAS A SIGNIFICANT MILESTONE IN THE BALANCING OF MR. T. THIS LED TO A NEW FORM OF MAN #HBA (HUMBLE BAD ASS).

form of man #HBA (Humble Bad Ass).

Do hormones have a conscience? Maybe, but testosterone is not one of them. On my drive home, thoughts of getting laid on the next date were dancing in my mind. Typical, right? That's how fast guys are capable of moving on from dismissal or distressing situations. Put an opportunity for sex out there, and whatever happened before fades into the background.

Getting over things fast is one thing, but we do have memories and can be sensitive. It took me a couple of weeks before I ventured back into that bar, fearing she'd put posters up about my inadequacies of the episode. Naturally, we bumped into each other, and not surprisingly she was quite decent.

I found out later, she was having a relationship with the bartender, an ex-pro athlete. I wondered whether he got to sleep over, but I never asked. Looking back, it was an experience, ie. #HBA, that altered my approach to casual relationships. This is clear evidence on how our society was evolving not only sexually, but out there in the real world too. Brazen women were now tasting power and control way beyond what they'd previously enjoyed, and men had to adjust. Clearly, testosterone was on the sacrificial altar.

But enough about my shortcomings, let's get back to the general population. From the seventies to the turn of the twenty-first century, men have been perplexed with what is acceptable when attempting to attract a woman. For a long time, you didn't know whether to open a door for a lady or not. If you did, she might thank you and smile … or scowl and insist on doing it herself.

Woman wanted equality, and the "rubber band principle" took over. That's the one where things get overdone before they come back to normal. It left a baffled path to all who became uncertain of where the art of picking up a woman and

> A SIGNIFICANT NUMBER OF WOMEN HAVE REVERTED TO LIKING THEIR MEN TO BE MEN AGAIN.

Mr. T fit in.

As we approach the second decade of the twenty-first century, those extremes have moderated. A significant number of women have reverted to liking their men to be men again. They want chivalry. Birth control has been around for a long time now, and the traditional male hunt is more or less back in vogue. However, the past sixty years were just long enough to leave most men feeling a lot more insecure.

Fact is, women wanted, and received, a fairer shot at equality. However, now they die earlier of heart attacks, stress-related cancers, and all those other nasty ailments that once were reserved for men. But they also got pay increases, job security, political positions, and CEO power. Are they further ahead now than before? The jury is still deliberating on that one.

The thing is, women still get pregnant. They have no option in this area. This fact forces them to deal with relationships and male sexual behavior from a completely different perspective. Nine months of growing out of your clothes, looking in the mirror, and peeing every twenty minutes takes its toll. During this ordeal, even though the husband is sympathetic, she watches him eat, drink, and carry on without a care. And once she gives birth and her mammary glands are stuck in the infant's mouth for another few months, we can see why their vocabulary tends to include words like, "bastards, irresponsible assholes, and oversexed freeloaders." I can see their point!

There's the anger rearing its ugly head again, but that's a book that has to come from a lady's point of view. I'm definitely not qualified. So let's stay with our prognosis of how men are focused on harnessing their T.

***

In the post-teenage mating environment, men have to size up the prize much faster, and have more tricks up their sleeve if they want to score. So let's take a look at the college-bound male, where there are a multitude of opportunities to have encounters with women.

These prospects happen in all sorts of mixed venues, such as campus pubs, coffee shops, libraries, coed dorms, study halls, and unlimited social events. Of course, our semi-promiscuous woman could be looking for her prince in shining armor too, but we all know what's going to happen after the hunter captures his or her prey.

> PUT A MIXED BUNCH OF SEMI-DRUNK TWENTY-YEAR-OLDS IN AN UNSUPERVISED AREA, AND THERE WILL BE SEX.

There are lots of one-night or one-weekend stands that punctuate the post-teenage sexual playground. No one perpetuates this behavior better than our colleges and universities. Half-naked and half-inebriated coed dorms, frat houses, and the general lack of restrictions on both sides seeking sexual freedom are the perfect breeding grounds for promiscuity.

Put a mixed bunch of semi-drunk twenty-year-olds in an unsupervised area, and there will be sex. That's pretty much a guarantee. So the man who is on the prowl has lots of low hanging fruit from which to choose. Sophomores and seniors typically pounce on freshman who are looking for acceptance and willing to do a lot to get it.

Typically, during those years, by the time the act of sex is over, the relationship is already at a crossroads. Intentions might have been honorable in the beginning, but by the time the sun rises, the relationship has dwindled significantly. What began as an emotionally charged, hormone-driven encounter the night before ends as quickly as it started. Both parties wake up the next day to face reality. They're sober, in broad daylight, and can clearly see that their partner isn't as perfect as they had thought the previous night.

"You'll call me, right?" She asks, knowing that it will never happen. She realizes she shouldn't have been so easy.

"Of course." His testosterone snickers, regrouping after the victory. "Text me your name and number. I'm going for a shower."

Here's the reality. The hunt is over. T has completed its mission. Time to regenerate and move on.

Of course, the total reverse is just as likely. The girl may pick up a guy, take him back to her place, and then dump him in the morning. Either way, it's casual sex. We've all seen it, done it, and have the T-shirt. No need to babble further.

> HUMANS ARE THE ONLY SPECIES WHERE BOTH SEXES CAN INITIATE, AND THIS LEADS TO CONFUSION AND DISAPPOINTMENT.

We should note here that in majority of the animal kingdom, courtship is very specific. Either the male or the female takes the lead and sets the rules for intercourse. There are no toys, variance in procedure, or a multitude of positions. That way nothing gets confused.

Humans are the only species where both sexes can initiate, and this leads to confusion and disappointment. Then there are the plethora of preferences each partner may have when having sex. For Pete's sake, these demands can put a ton of anxiety on both parties to perform or be fulfilled. This can lead to even more disappointment. Who wants to feel inferior in bed? No one! So it's a natural reason to move on.

Most of the time, our society could care less about procreation. It's all about pleasure because sex for us is a recreational activity. Both men and women are guilty.

So it makes sense that the college student behaves the way he does. The college campus offers a prime playground for Mr. T to exert his influence. And you know what? He's right. And I don't think girls who are just as sexually active can disagree. You may be trying hard to bond with the boys, but in the end there's just too much temptation, competition, and willing partners. Tell me I'm wrong!

Meanwhile, back on campus, our testosterone-driven male tries in vain to satiate his sexual desires. He may work through a hundred fantasies, but in the end it's all about conquering. The result of this behavior is that he will spend far less time searching for "the one." Results? The more women he seduces with this casual approach, the more numb he becomes toward a long-term relationship.

But it's not all negative. By sleeping around he may acquire skills and the ability to find a compatible candidate for a long-term relationship. Sex is no different than any other thing one learns. You avoid the ones you're not compatible with and keep the better ones around.

***

According to college statistics, about 45 percent of full-time students have sex with multiple partners on a regular basis. That leaves 55 percent that don't have much casual sex, but they are far from out in the cold. These "normal" guys and girls still bed one to five lovers over the course of their secondary education.

Contrary to what most women think, not all men are only after sex. In fact, as a result of the pressures of living in our society, most men go into casual relationships hoping that next woman might be the one. Most are honestly trying to get to know the girl before the seduction takes place, and in most cases it's mutual. And let's be clear here: Both parties are open for a deeper relationship, but at such an impressionable age, sex gets in the way. In the premarital world, sexual inquisitiveness and satisfaction rates way higher than making babies or the fear of STDs. Factor in internet porn, Tinder, Fling and Match or live chats where bodies are put on display, and it's easy to see why sex is so pervasive.

For most of those post-secondary days, raging T drags the poor boy way out of balance. He juggles the idea of finding a mate versus finding someone to have sex with. The more women you have, the further away the concept of marriage becomes.

However, after a while all of his sexual triumphs begin to become mechanical, whether he admits it or not. This puts pressure on the responsible side of his brain to take up the search for "Miss Perfect."

> EVEN THOUGH FEW MEN WILL ADMIT IT, SEX FOR THE SAKE OF SEX CAN BECOME BORING.

Even though few men will admit it, sex for the sake of sex can become boring. It can awaken the inherent nesting gene inside his head and cause him to seek that total package of good looks, sex, and great personality. Therefore, he starts to think about longer relationships, especially when some of his buddies start to tie the knot.

This revelation is not a fireworks kind of explosion in his mind. It's very subconscious. Waking up alone, or with a different woman starts to lose its appeal. Macho men will deny it, but it's true nonetheless. The different names, idle chat, and empty promises starts to weigh on his conscience. This is when men begin to imagine what marriage might be like. If only they could find the perfect woman.

Then, out of the blue, he meets HER. Instantly, there's a different kind of connection. Everything is different, and not just the sex. They go away together for a weekend. They watch old movies, go for nature walks, and don't want their time together to end. The days pass by quickly, and he doesn't even think about his buddies. When she falls asleep, he stares at her face, strokes her hair, and watches her breathe. Is this heaven?

She wakes up looking better than she did when she fell asleep. She makes the bed, then whips up a meal from nothing. He pours the wine and sets the table. They share a candlelight dinner. She clears the dishes, which they wash together, and she does the laundry. It doesn't matter what they're doing, so long as they're doing it together.

You know, many women love to mother their men, and I know that comment will upset some people. But is it not true?

Like it or not, it's what really happens. All men know, like, and desire this state of pampering. Most women want to show their special guy their domestic side in order hook the poor boy. This is Attraction 101 and proof of our genetic makeup. It's been around since the first time we stood up on two legs. So there's no use denying it, because you know it's true.

Back to our couple. When the boy starts to appreciate domesticated things, he gets the urge to settle down and share it with his lady. But hold on now, there's no hurry. We still have lots of time to explore options. Once their weekend getaway is over, it's back to the classroom with its mixed population where anything can happen. Maybe they continue to date, and even get married. Hopefully their story ends well. Sometimes, it's just another revolving door and that's okay too.

I'm sure most men can remember a magnificent lover, or amazing sex partner, that moved their universe. Would you agree? I bet their names and fragrances are still fresh in your mind, and if you close your eyes, you can still feel the rapturous sensations you experienced with her. However, most of us don't end up with those girls because we found them in during a time when we were playing the field. You can bet your last dollar that if you had the chance to be with one of them right now, you would jump on it. Even if you're happily married, I bet it would be tempting.

Alas, what's in the past is in the past, and where you are is where you are—and that's that. It's a lesson we learn on the road to controlling T and balance. Namely, you appreciate that something has come and gone, that it's over and cannot be recreated on any level. You learn to move on, and this is good for optimizing your attitude and attaining balance.

Of course, some of us try in later years to relive the glory of those bygone experiences. Mostly, they are met with disappointing results. For example, you don't want to be at a disco club in faded jeans when you're forty-five, or be backpacking through Europe either. Get the experience at the age you're supposed to and live it to the fullest. If you go on living in the past, you will find it very difficult to find balance. But a lot of men hold onto memories that brought them something good.

Maybe that's why they keep singing "Maggie Mae," "Can't Get No Satisfaction," "American Woman" and a host of other songs from "back in the day."

I'm sure you get the point. Live your life and sow your oats during the time you're supposed to do it. Accomplish what you must when you are young, then move on to the next level. Keep the good things with you, toss out the bad, and you may achieve peace. Life is a series of diverse battles. Some you win, some you lose. The most important thing is to play and get better. This is relevant to you sowing your wild oats. Before we drift too far away from the topic of this chapter, let's get back to it.

***

> AGE IS NOT A FACTOR, AND WHEN WE WANT SEX, WE WILL STRETCH THE TRUTH, LEAP TALL BUILDINGS, AND WALK MILES TO GET IT.

We've already said sex in young people is rampant. As you pass through those years, you have to balance your emotions based on who you slept with the night before and who you will sleep with next.

I could go on and on about how clever a man becomes when he is on the hunt for sexual fulfillment, but why beat a dead horse. The statistics indicate that the average man has a sexual thought three times more often than women. Need I say more? We are animals who lust, period. Age is not a factor, and when we want sex, we will stretch the truth, leap tall buildings, and walk miles to get it.

Back to coed copulation. Is there any doubt in these early

years when testosterone is exploding through our veins that young men are out of balance? They may have some inkling of becoming a doctor, lawyer, bricklayer, CEO, or veterinarian, but for the most part the topics that infiltrate the male mind in his post-teen years are sports, sex, cars, sex, booze, sex, bikinis, sex, video games, and spring break. That sums it up in no specific order.

Here are some final thoughts. At this point in the sex life of most male students, there's not much depth (call that responsibility) coming from the cerebral side of his brain.

<u>Scoreboard</u>: Early stages of spreading his seed

Testosterone: Here for the long haul. Mothers and fathers, protect your daughters.

Balance: Sports, cars, sex, booze, sex, broads, bikinis, video games, sex, spring break, sex on the beach, and beer with sex. You figure it out.

Score for this chapter: Completely out of balance

Total: Out of balance: 3   In balance: 1

*A footnote here. The lad is one-fourth of the way through his life, and (according to our scorecard) testosterone pretty much keeps him out of balance 75 percent of the time. Men are struggling to get control—something women should empathize with. You may fight the uphill battle to cure your man of these symptoms, but the odds are against you. Better to talk about each other's issues in a civilized fashion. Work together to find hormonal balance through the expressive and turbulent times you both live in.

CHAPTER 8

THE HUNT FOR MATERIAL SUPREMACY

All work and no play is not good for your sanity.

Graduation! I've got my degree in hand. School is a luke-warm memory, and the world is at my feet. It's time to get a decent job so I can start to amass the things I had when I was living with my parents, only my stuff will be bigger and better!

Wait a minute. Did you see the freaking price tag on that ultra-thin 3D TV? That's two months' salary. The super-cool sports car I've been eyeing is over eighty grand. How the hell is someone supposed to afford these things, pay rent, eat, and date? I don't get it. However, there are guys out there who are living large, so I guess it's possible. To that end, I've created a plan.

I'm going to use a couple of those credit cards I recently

acquired to put a deposit on some furniture. I can get a modular couch, two easy chairs, and a dining room set with no payments until next year. It's a sweet deal. I'll put a couple hundred in a savings account each payday, and when it comes due, I'll pay it. No problem.

To pimp up my place a tad more, I can afford to use the cash advance option in my checking account to buy that HDTV and pay it back over time too. The minimum payment won't kill me, and I figure within a few months I'll have the TV paid off. The chicks will be impressed, and my buddies can eat their hearts out. My place will rule, and I'll put an offer on the BMW within a year. I might have to cut back a little socially (Aha! Balance sneaks into his vocabulary.) But my plan is genius.

> THIS MENTALITY IS THE BANE OF OUR YOUNG MAN.

This mentality is the bane of our young man. Cheap credit (he learns about interest after paying the minimum for six months and not seeing the principle go down) can kill you. The bills just keep pouring in. He uses the small amounts of extra cash to pay car insurance, electricity, cable, internet, cell phone, groceries, and a few nights out at the bar from time to time. After all, you gotta pay for the drinks if you wanna get the chicks.

When the free year expires on the furniture, his bulletproof plan is riddled with holes. Presto change-o, he's deeper in debt than he ever thought possible, and panic sets in. But hold on, this is a good thing and is another example of the rubber band principle. To survive, he has to put together a budget and stick to it. He learns discipline, which collides with both Mr. T and balance. As a result, he realizes that there are restrictions in life, which in time will force him to balance his needs and desires.

Make no mistake. The temptation to get everything at once is great when one starts to make money. But without restraint, it will take the poor boy years to recover. The accumulation phase puts an enormous toll on today's youth because they are commercially bombarded with what they should have versus what they can afford. Almost everyone lives above their means in our society. It's what keeps the economy going.

***

One young man was visiting my home and shaking his head. He had come from a fairly well-off family and was out there struggling to make ends meet. He confessed that his parents had brought him up with most of the luxuries that baby boomers provide for their children. He struggled with this disconnect, namely to grasp the actual price of an object in relation to the ultimate cost of obtaining his parents' standard of living.

While he was growing up, it was a given that his folks brought in the money for food, clothing, computers, pools, hot tubs, and so on. He had never been without any of those things. It never occurred to the child that it took his parents twenty to forty years of hard work, careful planning, saving, and investing to achieve the lush home with all of its amenities. Let's face it. It's a shock for children when they finally realize what the good life costs. What to do?

After completing their education, every man should have "cash is king" branded on his forehead. If he lives within his means for the first few years, he has a much better chance at conquering the mountain of debt he will tackle going forward. Stability and financial control can make a huge swing in the pendulum of balance and the control of Mr. T.

Some never make it. They crash and burn in their early lives by overspending their paycheck. The result is a nasty fall. However, our story is an optimistic one. So for the most part, our young man muddles his way through those early years with an average amount of debt. He controls his urges to overindulge. He doesn't quite reach the material supremacy he once thought possible, but he has enough to satisfy his needs.

***

Next, let's take a look at one typical mogul to-be. We'll call him Johnny. He goes to his parents for Sunday dinner. While swallowing a piece of turkey and sinking his fork into the garlic mashed potatoes soaked with gravy, our hero throws out the question, "Dad? Can I borrow a few bucks?" The primary reason he attends Sunday dinner is that they're free, and a good home-cooked meal is not available in his overextended abode.

"How much, and what do you need it for?" the caring but cautious father shoots back.

The boy chomps on a sour pickle and mumbles. "Couple hundred. I'm really trying to pay down my Visa."

Mom offers. "Good for you. That's very responsible. High-interest rates are murder."

"You're not kidding." The boy reaches for a glass of wine and takes a slug.

Dad gets right to the point. "How much do you owe?"

Johnny dips his potatoes into the gravy. "Um … remember when I bought the furniture for my living room?"

"Uh-huh." Dad reaches for his own wine glass.

"Well, the principal is due this month."

"I thought you were saving from each paycheck to pay that off."

The boy shrugs and tries to look vulnerable. "Well, I had a few unexpected bills."

"Like what?" Dad keeps on him.

"Oh honey," the wife interjects, "it's' only a couple of hundred. He'll pay you back."

"Like what?" Dad repeats.

The son brightens up. "You know I didn't have a vacation since I started working, and I got a really good deal on that all-inclusive trip to Mexico last month. Some of my savings went there."

"How much is some?" Dad relentlessly prods on.

Johnny has stopped eating. His cheeks are flushed. "All of it."

Whether or not Dad coughs up the cash is irrelevant. The point being, our young man has to exercise some kind of spending restraints in order to grow. He needs a system, and both parents can help by offering a bit of tough love.

> I'M SURE THIS TYPE OF CONVERSATION HAPPENS IN MOST FAMILIES AT ONE TIME OR ANOTHER.

I'm sure this type of conversation happens in most families at one time or another. The parents love their boy, but the rules of spending weigh on him as he tries to live, love, spend, save, eat, entertain, and get laid. You see, as one grows and tastes the good life, the list of new enticements becomes ever larger as he watches his buddies amassing their stuff.

So our hero learns that in order to have certain things, he must learn sacrifice and control. This gives him financial and emotional stability and puts him on the road to survival. How does Mr. T fare while he's learning restraint? Don't worry about that pesky varmint. He's in cruise control and never misses an opportunity to remind our hero he supposed to be breeding.

During these early years, the young man oscillates between keeping his boyish habits of playing video games, watching sports, and dating while trying to establish himself in the workplace as a responsible adult. At the office, he is learning to deal with authority while in his spare time he tries to keep his freedoms and hunt down women. He may have a career that affords him the opportunity for personal input, or he may have a mundane job that requires physical labor. Either way, we have a similar situation to when the boy was back in high school, except now he has his own place and is tackling the rigors of self-reliance. Once again, unless he becomes an alcoholic, sexual deviant, or hits the financial wall, he has it pretty good. He wants a lot, and he's diligently working his way toward his goals. Stress levels are tolerable, and he's accumulating some cool things.

Over the next few years, he will climb the corporate ladder, learn about the stock market, MLM schemes and investing, get a better car, clothes and acquire some art. He'll also move up to a king-sized bed complete with matching pillows and Egyptian cotton sheets. He'll also get his finances in shape for the next challenge. That would be a longer-lasting relationship, complete with a detached home, downtown or in the suburbs. The future will confront Mr. T with more difficult challenges. But don't sweat it. History has made him very resilient.

Before he knows it, the boy'll be thirty, and with that monumental birthday, certain hopes and dreams he's held in his mind since graduating will either begin to expand or decline. Before we go there, we need to stop the clock and review some very important aspects of the male personality. These traits are, by and large, typically male and are instrumental in managing Mr. T during those high contamination years. So let's plod on.

Scoreboard: As the hunt for material supremacy begins

Testosterone: At par with what he's trying to accumulate and accomplish. His mind and sex drive are beginning to take separate paths as his pursuit of the "good things in life" phase begins.

Balance: For the most part, he's under control and once again he gets the benefit of doubt.

Score for this chapter: In balance

Total: Out of balance: 3   In balance: 2

CHAPTER 9

COMPETITIVE VERSUS THOUGHTFUL

Kill or be killed. Competition is a basic fact of life and has been since time began. Man had to be stronger, faster, and smarter to survive. He never had to go far to find an enemy someone who wanted his food, cave, weapon, fire, or woman. Eventually, man created games, and even those meant winning at any cost. Even the Olympic Games were created for man to showcase his competitive skills. But long before that, man was continually in a fight for his life.

We flash back to a historical view. Since the earliest origins of Homo sapiens, the male species dominated because of physical strength, logic, and a keen sense of direction. He had to compete for and protect everything in his world or die trying. By hook or by crook, he controlled his food, shelter, weapons, mate, and even his offspring. Quick thinking and muscle power ensured his continued existence.

Time marched on. Along came the Greeks, Romans, Egyptians, Galileo, Einstein, the rise of industrialization, and Nobel Prizes. Still, not much changed in terms of male characteristics. In 99.9 percent of the cases, man was the leader of the pack. Even within emerging monolithic religions such as Christianity and Catholicism, which focus on a single masculine God, men were typically the only sex worthy to be prophets and to speak to God directly. Women could only talk to God through their husbands.

> IN 99.9 PERCENT OF THE CASES, MAN WAS THE LEADER OF THE PACK.

Each of these religions had a supreme male at the head of the organization: Jesus, Mohammed, Buddha, or the pope. These figures of male power upheld male domination. Even the Bible said, "God created man in his image." This gave him a superiority complex too. Men led wars, science, and even the arts. It was men who ascended to become extremely well paid athletes and heads of state. They conquered in the bedroom *and* held the earning power. They even led in the great kitchens of the world. Man was expected to lead, and this remains essentially unchanged. Mostly, this is all due to his physical strength compared to the weaker female. However, no one can be on top forever. So where was his Achilles heel, the one battle that his physical superiority could not win?

It was the battle of the brain. Man cannot outfox the opposite sex.

No matter how tough our hombre is, he has never been able to function properly when love smitten by the Cleopatras, Marilyn Monroes, Scarlett Johanssons, or Jessica Biels of the world. With all his testosterone and physical superiority, it's a fight he can never really win. However, man started out on top, and that's where he still struggles to be.

I think the last couple hundred thousand years have instilled a long tradition of man being at the front of the herd. Let's not kid ourselves here; it's an affinity for power that is difficult for men to give up. After all, it's hard enough for men to take orders from other men, much less a woman. Think back to the first time a woman ordered her man to do a task. If the act wasn't motivated by lust or love, then I'm pretty sure her request was not granted, and it was likely an insult to a man.

Sure, there are a handful of good examples out there, such as Joan of Arc and Margaret Thatcher, but can you imagine Madonna, Angelina Jolie, or Oprah ordering today's man into battle? Got to think about that one!

Consider this, would you go to war for a female president if she wasn't backed up by a predominantly male government and four-star generals? Take a look at the United Nations. What's the ratio of male and female delegates? Women have sometimes dotted the landscape, but the majority has always been male. The Supreme Court has only one female, but there was a recent push to add another. The point here is that it would be another instance of a woman taking a man's traditional job. They get stronger, while men suck it up and become weaker. All in the name of equality.

***

Getting back to our opening comparison, so far I've pounded the competitive nature of man into your head, but be patient, the contemplative, compassionate man society is pushing for is lurking in the shadows. He's just shy and afraid to make himself known.

For him to get over the hump, we should compare how we equate the treatment of our women to those of Eastern cultures. The men in this country have been a beacon to the world regarding equality. Some Eastern cultures, not so much. Check out the differences. They are staggering.

It's generally acknowledged that there are many cultures across the world that value women about as much, or a little better, than a dog. In these cultures women are oppressed, and very often abused in a number of ways. They have no chance of ever achieving any level of independence, financial or otherwise. Men control their fate, and they have nearly no say whatsoever. Sadly, much of this behavior is protected by laws in those countries or is sanctioned by religious dogma. It's insane, and women's groups on our continent would make fast work of the guilty parties, but they shouldn't try it on foreign soil. If they do that, they will soon find out what inequality is all about.

> ON THIS SIDE OF THE OCEAN, NORTH AMERICAN MEN HAVE MADE A CONCERTED EFFORT TO LIBERATE AND EDUCATE OUR WOMEN SO THEY CAN ACHIEVE ANYTHING A MAN CAN.

On this side of the ocean, North American men have made a concerted effort to liberate and educate our women so they can achieve anything a man can. This state of mind happens on our soil more than anywhere else on this planet, and men should be given kudos for encouraging our women and following through to make it happen.

Now whether our women will admit the role men had in their achievements is another question. They can argue against this premise and claim that women are solely responsible for all their gains. However, look at all the other countries where women are oppressed. You don't think for a moment that those women want what our women have? Sure, they do. They just can't get it. They have no hope because their men will not allow it.

There has to be a reason why our society has emerged as the unequivocal leader in women's rights. The answer is because our men endorsed and fought alongside our women to achieve status. You can argue about where women got these freedoms and opportunities from for as long as you like, but man's acquiescence of power and his ability to share is the main reason and the truth. These are traits that come from his desire to protect and shelter his physically weaker partner or the mother of his offspring. So let's give credit for women's rights and equality where credit is due. Men deserve as much or more recognition than women, and I've begun to show you why.

But let's get back to how men struggle to deal with competitiveness (our natural state) versus thoughtfulness (a more learned and civilized state).

You see, something happened when Columbus sailed across the ocean and gave those foolhardy voyagers a place to colonize from sea to sea. The New World led to new ideas. Women were initially brought over specifically to be wives and bear children, but there was a significant difference in how these women were received.

Coming from their traditional European lifestyle to the harsh realities of resettling, the women took on heftier roles in this brave new world. Thankful for their participation, the men needed them and encouraged them to be strong and independent. This resulted in letting women make more decisions around the homestead. When they stood up for themselves, the men gave in instead of squashing them. It empowered women in their men's eyes and gave them stature.

God bless a strong, hardworking woman who can take charge. Most men recognize that there's something very cool about being able to wrestle physically and mentally with your woman on a more or less equal basis. It's very sexually stimulating, especially if she almost wins. You feel like you have the best of both worlds—a girl you can be tough with, yet when you want to make love, she's this soft, sexy thing that you adore. If you have this kind of relationship, it is extremely balancing because you don't have to look to others for mutually exhilarating things to do. But let's get back to the plot.

> GOD BLESS A STRONG, HARDWORKING WOMAN WHO CAN TAKE CHARGE.

In those wild days of settling a new land, women took on tasks like skinning game and helping around the barn. Hell, they even loaded up a musket and killed the odd rabbit or coyote. Men saw them as true cohorts in the rebuilding and not just childbearing "Stepford Wives." They were earning their stripes, and men admired them for their grit. This caused our men to be open minded toward a different kind of acceptance. He allowed his partner more say in matters that concerned the couple and made sure their children respected their mother too.

Sure, there was still a bias toward the weaker, prettier sex, but the seeds for equality were in the ground. This new breed of Western woman took the opportunity to water that seed and sprout some foliage in the bright sunshine. By the mid-twentieth century, men saw women not as the competition but as an ally against the harshness of the times. Men accepted the change; in fact, they thought it was kinda cute. Voila! So women were on their way. Of course there were obstacles, but the end justifies the means. It's no coincidence that Michelle Obama was as powerful as her husband, even without holding office.

If you think of competitiveness as an opposite to thoughtfulness, then what changed? Man's cutthroat combativeness has been bludgeoned to death. If he gives mercy or leniency, he shows weakness, which is not a good trait for a conqueror. On the battlefield, there's no time for rational appraisals of whether the guy shooting or swinging an ax at you is anything else but the enemy. You kill first, ask questions later.

So where did thoughtfulness come from? Why are North American men more open to equality than historical types like Attila the Hun or other barbarians? The answer, and the most profound reason why our hero stands up for and is more thoughtful toward his women, turns out to be love. That's right. It's love or the pursuit of love that changed things.

> WHY ARE NORTH AMERICAN MEN MORE OPEN TO EQUALITY THAN HISTORICAL TYPES LIKE ATTILA THE HUN OR OTHER BARBARIANS?

The desire for the attention of a desirable woman, lustful or not, triggered this modification in mentality. "True love" changes the way we treat our women. This is not to say that Eastern or European cultures do not love, but they also have a long tradition of polygamy, arranged marriages, or joint agreements for money and power. There is a blind-eye perception, and "openly secret" love affairs that bring some shame or scandal to the family, but for the most part it's accepted. So it's not such a big price to pay. And the beat goes on.

It's important to note here that, in the New World, man began to choose partners solely for love and married them regardless of their social standing. This ratcheted up the pressure on our hero to be more open to female needs and desires. Do you think for a moment that "living happily ever after with Prince Charming" came from a woman? Of course not. It came from Oscar Wilde's perception of how women wanted to view their knight in shining armor. Man is not set up for extensive wooing and courtship. He's just as happy in a sweat suit or jeans when he is pursuing sex as he is living happily ever after.

> WHEN NORTH AMERICAN MAN PURSUES A WOMAN FOR TRUE LOVE, HE ELEVATES HER EVEN ABOVE HIMSELF.

Men are not as shallow as we may seem because there are other forces at work. When North American man pursues a woman for true love, he elevates her even above himself. Thus, the softer side of man blossoms, along with the willingness to put her up on that pedestal. And our hero's new tempered, romantic side counteracts his competitive side. When the boy is lovesick, T stays at home and is on a "need to react" basis, but there are a couple of other hormones that pick up the slack. These hormones don't cause a man to fight or lust.

I became acquainted with these two hormones back in my university days. Both hormones have stuck in my brain ever since. They are dopamine and phenethylamine. Dopamine gives you a similar feeling as cocaine. Every time you see your love, you get a shot and it's addictive. That means you can't wait to see her again and again and again. Phenethylamine increases your heartbeat, causes you to breathe faster, makes your palms sweat, and your cheeks and genitals get an extra burst of blood. Plus, you feel happier. So with these hormones substituting for Mr. T, the courting male spends his time in heavenly bliss, waiting for the next glimpse or touch of the woman he loves.

The flipside of love could be called jealousy, which turns out to be more powerful than any weapon. Love or jealousy can bring a man to his knees with bliss or pain. Rejection from a woman who doesn't love back can cause more destruction than any nuclear bomb. These factors weigh heavily on man's ability to achieve balance. Therefore, to be in balance revolves around being in a state of love. One must love oneself and the one he's with. If either scenario is out of step, balance falters and testosterone comes back with a vengeance, both in sexual need and aggression.

We've all been in love, right? Teenage love can make any boy do irrational things to get the attention of a girl. The first cavemen fight was probably over a piece of food. The second was probably over a woman.

> ONLY THE
> RESTORATION OF
> LOVE CAN REKINDLE
> BALANCE AND GET
> T BACK UNDER
> CONTROL.

Balance revolves around man's response to love or rejection, whether it's in relationships or at work. We've all known someone who had the "divorce from hell." We've all experienced, to some degree, being scorned, and we all know how screwed up we get when our relationship is not firing on all cylinders. It's during these times that T's aggressive behavior takes precedent. He becomes a lifeless object and strikes out with barbaric cruelty, even at the ones he may love. Only the restoration of love can rekindle balance and get T back under control.

So what has changed while equality was creeping up the stairs? Liberal feminists and emancipated women may argue that previously suppressed women sacrificed their lives, or existence, in order to achieve women's current state of equality. However, to a certain extent, women's gains have been at the erosion of man's historical status. I'm not debating right or wrong. I'm only saying that women have been allowed to flourish because men have backed off and encouraged them to do their thing.

Rebellious women are out there in all parts of the world, but it is mainly in our society that women have been able to shimmy their way up the Conga line. The Law of the Jungle states that any repressed race or species can only be allowed to survive and evolve if the ruling forces or the general masses relaxes its position and agrees to consent.

History documents this observable fact related to class, race, and sex distinction since Eve took a bite from that apple. More "equalizing events" took place through the French and Russian revolutions, aboriginal rights, the abolition of slavery, the end of apartheid, and even the election of the first African American president. Granted, barriers had to be broken down for women to rise to historical heights. But it has been largely due to man's focused commitment to subdue his testosterone and become thoughtful and compassionate.

You see, if man is left to his own recognizance, he will rape, pillage, conquer, and kill other men, women, and even children. It's in his nature, pure and simple. Check out any history book. Basically, he only needs to eat, be sheltered, and have sex. However, when women are welcomed into his life with love, man takes on a more subdued persona. Beside her, he becomes a better man. He is willing to negotiate, share, and even die.

In loving relationships, his testosterone-influenced outbreaks are tempered by his need to coexist with his woman. This influences a man's "tank mentality" by subduing Mr. T. Thus, he becomes more sensitive and gravitates to what are typically called feminine traits, such as caring, compassion, and sensitivity.

I see most men reading this begin to squirm, but it gets even better, because in order to coexist in "equality's world," you have to justify this new softer side to your buddies, hence the terms "hen-pecked" or "ball and chain." Let me put it into perspective.

Your woman asks, "What are you thinking?" When this question is first thrust upon our hero, he is likely in shock.

> IT IS THE MOST AMBIGUOUS YET PROFOUND QUESTION IN THE ENTIRE WORLD.

Here's the scenario. The man and woman have just settled into the sofa to watch television. A commercial comes on, she lays her head on his shoulder, looks up with a soul-searching look in her eyes, and hits him with that question. It thoroughly rattles him, and he enters the mystic world of the black hole.

It is the most ambiguous yet profound question in the entire world. To my knowledge, no man has ever asked it first.

What are you thinking right now?

The words hit him like a ton of bricks. "Jeeez, Louise," he

whispers, his brain scanning all four corners of his cerebellum for an intelligent response. This singular question has sent many a man scurrying for relationship exits.

"C'mon," she playfully purrs, nudging his cheek with her nose. "What's going on in that head of yours?"

Terror sets in. His eyes dart this way and that. "I'm wondering what *you're* thinking," he blurts out, stalling for time.

She pushes on. "Afraid to tell?" Of course, she's thinking oxytocin-influenced thoughts. She's thinking about how the relationship is evolving, and she wants confirmation, something with substance, something deep.

"I'm not afraid," T blurts out from within, but what he means is that he has no idea how to respond. His mind goes through the process. *We were having a nice time up until this.* His thoughts are churning, smoke coming from both ears. *I know she's looking for something cerebral, but the only thing deep I'm thinking about is how to get her in the right mood before this movie is over.* This may be somewhat overstated, but you get the drift.

***

Consider going into a football locker room, then sitting beside a two-hundred-fifty-pound linebacker. Our hero inches over close enough to almost touch the bigger guy, and the words leak out in a soft voice: "What are you thinking, Billy Bob?"

Billy Bob's eyes zoom in, his forehead furrowed like a plowed wheat field. "What the hell?" Billy Bob pulls his helmet on and gets up with a disgusted look on his face, mumbles something about kicking our hero's ass, and walks away.

"Right!" I nod to myself, hearing the sound of Billy's cleats as he clomps out of the room. I give my head a good shake.

What the hell was I thinking?

Getting back to the date, our guy needs to focus. This isn't a linebacker, and he can't tell her he's going to kick her ass. His brain is on fire. *What can I say so she won't think I'm shallow?*

You see, men don't automatically think in terms of why, when, where, or what unless there's an immediate obstacle to deal with. If confrontation is on the near horizon, his brain toughens up, and logical responses kick in. This is followed by the arrival of Mr. T, and adrenaline starts pumping. However, when he's relaxed, his guard is down, and his thoughts become reduced to simple things like eating, gadget hunting, sports, fixing something, or recreational things like dating. There's no danger in watching a movie with a girl, so Mr. T is focused on only one thing.

Dating is an anomaly for most men. They'd like to be that badass they think they are. (We all remember that women are drawn to bad boys.) But here's a girl you actually like being with. In fact, you'd rather be with her than most of your buddies.

Granted, dating her has primal rewards, and that is an important point too. As in the chapter on spreading his seed, our hero is forced to deal with a potential mate, but when we talk about the ramifications of a long-lasting relationship, he needs to bear down and be sensitive. Not only to her physical needs, but her mental ones as well. It puts a major pile of unknowns on the scale. We're talking about getting along over an extended period of time by making concessions, giving in, and even losing some arguments if you want to keep the relationship going. We're talking about giving up dimensions that define us as men, not to mention dealing with emotions.

Emotions aren't the kind of thing a man gets caught up in unless someone smashes into his car, or he loses at poker. I

> EMOTIONS AREN'T THE KIND OF THING A MAN GETS CAUGHT UP IN UNLESS SOMEONE SMASHES INTO HIS CAR, OR HE LOSES AT POKER.

mean, he's a doer, someone who takes action. Most of the time he's already doing whatever it is before he even thinks about doing it. It's spontaneous, a reflexive knee-jerk reaction. The words or deeds go off without dissecting the consequences.

You gotta admire that about our hero. He's rough, straight to the point, pretty much a blunt object. That is, until he meets a woman who asks these kinds of questions. With that said, he has to learn tact. For him, it's uncharted territory.

And that's exactly my point. North American man becomes chemically altered by the infusion of feminine qualities when he finds the woman he loves. Afterall, this is someone he could truly want to be with for a long time. Is it a bad or good thing? The jury is still out, but learning how to deal with emotions is one of the most profound stepping-stones to achieving balance and managing good ole T. For without this infusion of sensibility, man would flounder aimlessly as he has for centuries, eliminating everything in his path. But in our modern world, he must muster up a whole new palette of emotional qualities. These new entanglements constitute a continuation of what man has been striving for over the centuries.

As far back as the Roman Empire, Octavius Caesar proclaimed that Rome's men were nothing more than barbaric, lustful heathens until they began to listen to their women. Only then did Rome become a great and mighty power. So it seems that loving relationships are a key to balance and a more civilized existence.

> SO IT SEEMS THAT LOVING RELATIONSHIPS ARE A KEY TO BALANCE AND A MORE CIVILIZED EXISTENCE.

Our men have taken up the "equality" torch and handed it off, like a big relay race to all his brothers, white, black, yellow, or red. He's gone from being a bludgeoning, bombastic Neanderthal to a milder version because of the love he searches for. Being able to freely choose mates has forced our hero to mellow, and when he is mellow, he begins to think about his existence in an entirely different way. He becomes open to questions like, "How far will I go to protect my family ... my rights?" and "What are you thinking right now?"

Don't be surprised if men come up with some pretty succinct answers. Women who are mental equals inspire men to be better human beings. Once a man accepts a woman for her brains and abilities, he is on a course that can alter evolution in the most positive way. As a complementary unit, both sexes are able to excel as long as the woman is learning right alongside him too.

Scoreboard: Competitive versus thoughtful

Testosterone: Is in conflict while he fights this battle of amassing wealth, hunting women, and climbing the corporate ladder versus being a thoughtful, caring being.

Balance: His pursuit of "love" forces him toward a more giving and forgiving lifestyle, but the desire to get ahead urges him to be cutthroat and to take all he can get.

This chapter deals with a stage of life that can span decades as our hero struggles and learns about life. That said, balance depending on events will shape his world, marriage, and professional career in many directions. It's a wash, therefore no furthering of the score. The one thing we have learned here is in order for our man to be balanced, he must have *love* in his life.

Score for this chapter: Wash

Total: Out of balance: 3   In balance: 2

CHAPTER 10

FALLING IN AND OUT OF LOVE

This chapter is going to be short because the reality of falling in and out of love is cut and dried. You're either completely smitten … or you're not. There are no close calls when men fall in love. It's an all-or-nothing event just like grenades or pregnancy.

You might think this chapter is another no-brainer for testosterone, but you'd be wrong. You see, when a man falls in love, it actually has nothing to do with sex or dominance. In fact, it's quite the opposite 'cause we've already shown that ole Testy is on the sidelines.

Sex may be the catalyst or one of the by-products of love, but sex

> YOU SEE, WHEN A MAN FALLS IN LOVE, IT ACTUALLY HAS NOTHING TO DO WITH SEX OR DOMINANCE.

has nothing to do with actually falling in love. The result of the mental state of falling in love is that testosterone gets reassigned to deal with protection and anger.

Let me use some adjectives to describe our hero when he falls in love. *Mush*, as in his brain. *Blurred*, as in his ability to focus. *Confused*, as in his ability to make decisions. *Stunned*, as in his ability to function. But crystal-clear in his desire to be with a particular girl. I could toss out a few more adjectives related to futility, but the gravity of the situation makes the fool pretty much helpless. He's in a state of dysfunction. Incidentally, none of these sates of mind are related to Mr. T.

Love makes a man helpless (damn that dopamine), yet it makes him complete. It's confusing, but I can be more specific. When our hero becomes infatuated with a certain girl, he will do everything within his power to see her, be with her, touch her, and protect her. He is consumed—hook, line, and sinker. Nothing can stop him from wanting to be one with her. It's not the sex that brings the boy back to her doorstep. It's the desire to have her all to himself and to be all alone with her essence.

> HE WILL GIVE UP ALL HIS POWER, RICHES, AND BEST FRIENDS—AND EVEN HIS LONG-ESTABLISHED HABITS—TO SPEND A SOLITARY MOMENT OF BLISS WITH HER.

He will give up all his power, riches, and best friends—and even his long-established habits—to spend a solitary moment of bliss with her. He will rearrange his schedule, travel thousands of miles, pass up sporting events, and sacrifice all, just to hear her voice. If they have sex, it's for the moment, and however euphoric that experience might be, it's just another driving force that keeps him wanting to be in her presence.

It's the smell of her hair, sound of her voice, softness of her skin, the way she looks at you and a thousand other things that compel him to be in her company. He is totally out of control. The minutes and hours they are separated cannot pass fast enough until they are together again. She spellbinds him. This is the true litmus test of being in love.

If you've been there, I bet you are nodding in agreement. You will notice the total deficiency of sexual innuendo when one falls off the cliff in total unconditional and uncompromising love. So by definition, the role testosterone plays in falling in and out of love is minimal. It's everything else about her that makes you fall.

So to be blunt, if you falling in love is dependent upon the shape and allure of her body, then that's not love. That's lust, and we've already covered that quite well. So be brave and proud if you've found real love. You are a better man for finding it, acknowledging it, and preserving it. Pay no mind to what the other guys say. Believe me, if they could get a taste of what you have, they'd take it in a heartbeat. The hard part will be staying in love and learning how to keep things fresh and alive. (See chapter 16!)

***

Next, let's look at what happens when you fall out of love. Now this is what testosterone has been waiting for. Get outta the way, 'cause when a man's love is rejected, there's going to be an ass kicking somewhere. There'll be chaos, revenge, hostility, and more.

Well, it's just as we suspected—lack of love is the perfect

launch site for Mr. T. Without his queen, our hero reverts to the rape, pillage, and conquer mode while he licks his wounds. Beware and take cover during the rebound stage as our warrior tries to get back in the saddle. There may be some broken bones and promises that go along for the ride. Let's hope he can reset and find another to share his life with so civilization can continue on its upbeat course.

> WELL, IT'S JUST AS WE SUSPECTED— LACK OF LOVE IS THE PERFECT LAUNCH SITE FOR MR. T.

Testosterone and balance can both be tidied up as neatly as a Christmas present at the gift-wrapping station at every mall in America. Falling in love is bliss. It can control T while creating balance. It makes our hero a nice guy: compassionate, thoughtful, and happy. Take love away and our heathen returns to the battlefield with a pickaxe, shield, hammer, and bazooka.

We only have one piece of advice to give at this time. If you can't be with the one you love, then love the one you're with. It's a start! If man has neither, pick your weapon and run for cover.

Actually, we may have found one solution if all else fails. Try falling in love with a complete stranger. A New York psychologist, Professor Arthur Arun, who has been studying why people fall in love, asked his subjects to carry out these three steps.

- Find a complete stranger.

- Reveal to each other intimate details about your lives for half an hour.

- Then, stare deeply into each other's eyes without talking for four minutes.

It seems that after the 34-minute experiment, the doc found that many of his couples felt deeply attracted. In fact, two of his subjects later got married. Hey, it's worth a shot.

Scoreboard: Falling in and out of love

Testosterone: Really not a factor

Balance: Completely and totally out of his skin. When our hero is in love, he is one with the universe and nothing can defeat him. Alternatively, when he falls out of love, the testosterone and every cell in his body become infected with the Prime Directive. He reverts to a state of control, conquer, rape, and pillage.

Score for this chapter: Half and half, depending on his state of love. So it's a wash.

Total: Out of balance: 3   In balance: 2

CHAPTER 11

MARRIAGE MATERIAL

Hope begins once you've found your dream girl. Now, ole Mr. T is at a bit of a crossroad. He keeps the competition away (by fighting if necessary) and tickles your arousal levels while you express your infinite love. Finding a mate and mating with her is right up T's alley. How does the hunting for game and sex hormone react once the consummation is complete?

A gaggle of divorce lawyers were drinking at a local watering hole. One of the senior partners stood, glass in hand, addressing the group. "What are the four most expensive words in the English language?"

A junior litigator leapt up. The abrupt movement sent the head of his beer over the edge of his mug. It ran down his hand, dripping onto the floor. All eyes focused on the robust lad's face, who made sure he had everyone's attention before blurting out, "The four most expensive words in the English language are, 'I do and I'm leaving.'"

All the lawyers at the table stood up as one, clanged glasses, and spoke their mantra in unison. "Long live infidelity and irreconcilable differences." Then the senior partner slapped the young protégée on the back while the group openly roared their approval.

The point?

Divorce lawyers' material gains are due directly to man's failure to achieve balance through long-term relationships. You see, marriage, monogamy, or the ceremonial joining of two people is not tried and true. If it was, there'd be a step-by-step best seller, and divorce wouldn't exist. But the potential for separation starts the day you move in or share rent with the opposite sex. The beginning is easy. You are in the market for someone to compliment your life.

> YOU SEE, MARRIAGE, MONOGAMY, OR THE CEREMONIAL JOINING OF TWO PEOPLE IS NOT TRIED AND TRUE.

True, some cohabit for economical purposes to share expenses, but even these relationships are short lived if both parties have major differences. Hence, young couples join forces and play house in apartments or living quarters as a dry run for finding that one person who they'd like to share the "happily ever after" dream with.

So out you go, locked and loaded with Mr. T scavenging about for "the one." It's like it was on campus, except the girls are harder to find now that you are in the business world. You do the bar thing, the casual dating thing. Then you hit the ski clubs, supermarkets, and golf courses. Perhaps you venture into online dating. You have a few sexual partners. You fall in love, you fall out of love, you lust, but after all is said and done, if you don't find "the pick of the litter" you end up empty and frustrated.

All the money in the world only buys percentiles of happiness and nothing of love, although I'll admit copious amounts of cash lessens the blow of despair. But that said, piles of thousand-dollar bills cannot buy true love. That only comes from within when two people connect to each other—heart and soul.

When that happens, our monogamy-driven society demands that you enter into holy matrimony. This commitment to a one-on-one relationship ante ups your share of the "whole" life experience. You are now eligible for the minivan, the kids, the widescreen TV, the soccer and baseball games, ballet class, and all those school operettas. They are there for one purpose—to expose you to the wealth of experiences that lay in your ever-maturing path. These will edge you closer and closer to gratification in life, in which you find serenity, financial freedom, mastery over your testosterone, and ultimate balance.

***

Let's look at a young man's story. Let's call him Fast Eddie. He was twenty-six, a good friend of mine, and gearing into marriage mode. Ed had been dating since he was seventeen, lost his virginity a year after that, then went on to have a few short-term relationships. Paula had the honor of being his first long-term girlfriend. He let her believe that he'd slept with quite a few others and was experienced enough to settle down. It's the macho thing, even though he'd only had sex with a handful of women.

Naturally, because of the longer term and his age, this was his first perception of "true" love. They talked about marriage so much that some of their friends, including her mother, were already buying things for the wedding. A few of our buddies had tied the knot, and that only increased pressure to succumb.

One day, we were over at our friend Kenny's place playing street hockey. Mr. B, Ken's dad, was stick-handling right along with us. Even though he was in his late forties, he was like one of the guys. He was that rare kind of father you could say anything to and he wouldn't look at you like you were a moron. After the game was over, Ed was munching on hot dogs and potato salad next to Mr. B.

"Hey, Mr. B! How do you know if you've found the right one?" Ed asked, mustard leaking from the corner of his mouth.

Mr. B looked at Ed with a smirk. "Thinking about getting married?"

Ed chomped down on the wiener, piled high with sweet fried onions. "Why? You think I'm too young?"

"Age has got nothing to do with it." Mr. B took a swig of a Coke.

Ed went on, trying to paint the right picture. "We've been dating for a long time, and I love her." (When you add the "I love her" clause, it helps sell the idea.) He went on. "I really like being with her, and I'm pretty sure it's the real thing." Mr. B chewed while listening, so Ed kept talking. "But how do I really know she's the right one? How do I justify giving up all those other babes?"

"Your perception of being in love sounds a little suspect." Mr. B refilled his glass and waited until the fizz bubbled down. "How many girls have you been in love with?" he asked with a raised eyebrow.

"I don't know, but this is different," Ed said, suddenly serious.

"How many have you had sex with?"

"Enough."

"Uh-huh." Mr. B nodded, then pushed on. "Let's say you've been in love ten times. And let's pretend that all those loves happened in the present."

Ed cut him off. "I've put those out of my mind. I've matured, and I'm ready to settle down."

"Maybe so." Mr. B took another gulp. "But for argument's sake, let's say you could be with any one of those girls you previously loved, and she was the one you're thinking of marrying. Pick any one of them. Retrace how you felt at the height of that relationship."

That got Ed thinking about the best parts and good times he'd had with Barbara, Helen, Karen, Wendy, Connie, Jackie, Danielle, Lee, Susan, and Kate. Those were the girls that made up his "top ten" before Paula. "What should I be focusing on?"

"Why those relationships didn't last." Mr. B said, coming down hard on a cucumber.

The question instantly revived the worst parts of those past relationships and tossed out all the previously lovely memories about each girl. We saw the change in Fast Eddie's face and laughed.

Mr. B continued, "You see, in a relationship it's easy to remember the good until you're forced to look at the other side. The bitching, moaning, fighting, differences in opinion … that's where the test comes. But here's the thing. You're at the age of 'marriage material.' I bet if you were with any of your top ten, you'd be thinking about marrying each and every one of them, right?"

Ed thought deeply, recalling how each relationship had started out hot, and then injected them into his current time frame. "It's a possibility." He begrudgingly shrugged.

"Well, that's my point," Mr. B said. "Any man can marry

> ANY MAN CAN MARRY A WHOLE SLEW OF WOMEN DEPENDING ON TIME AND CIRCUMSTANCE AND HAVE DIFFERENT RESULTS.

a whole slew of women depending on time and circumstance and have different results. If you take your top ten girls and marry each one of them, your marriages would end up something like this. Five out of ten would be a disaster, and they would probably end quickly, just like what happened in the actual relationships.

"The next three would be tolerable and maybe you'd get by, but you wouldn't be totally satisfied. Then you get to the top two. Well, you may be lucky and find a woman who shares the same lifestyle as you, is a great lover, good cook, super mother, etc. You're deeply in love and it could stand the test of time. But if you find *that one,* that perfect one you respect, that you can be an equal with, then you'll achieve marital balance, and you won't care or even think about being with other women. This can only happen when she complements you and you complement her. This will be a relationship where you could both be together day and night, year after year.

"This is what I believe to be the definition of true love … and true friendship. When you have the same interests and goals over time, it can only get better. This doesn't mean either has to sacrifice friends, family, or job relationships and become hermits. It means that you both can bring out the best in each other while you live out your life. This ability to mingle, yet be one, is the most important aspect to any relationship, especially marriage. It has to be there and get nurtured through the years. It also doesn't mean that the marriage will go in a straight line. There's always going to be good and bad years."

He dropped his glass into the sink and grabbed his hockey gloves. "Do you and your girl have a lot in common, and do you have a plan for your future?"

We stood by the fridge as Mr. B left the room.

Ed was forced into visualizing what he and Paula had in common. He was thinking out loud. "That made a lot of sense. But if we both had the same interests and we did everything together, wouldn't we get bored with each other, and wouldn't it take all the spontaneity out of the mix? The unknown and adventure of the future was a main reason why we wanted to marry, so we could experience life and grow together."

Mr. B's advice created a kind of indigestion problem. Like almost all potential newlyweds, Ed and Paula had no long term concrete plan, and he could see how their growth could be affected depending on a wide range of outcomes. His analysis drenched Ed with new pressure. Getting married and starting to build a life with this woman was immense. All of a sudden, he felt as if he was underneath Niagara Falls with millions of gallons of water pouring over him.

I also thought long and hard about Mr. B's advice. Inside my own heart, I knew he was probably right. Ed confided that his and Paula's universal goals hadn't been discussed at much length, other than playing house until they'd have kids and so forth.

It also occurred to me that in my own life, in fact, I didn't have much of a plan. What if I were in Ed's position? I hadn't given marriage much thought other than the usual suspects of paying the mortgage, having kids, working, bringing home the bacon, going on cool vacations, etc. In my current relationship, I was in the throes of my own "Marriage Material" predicament.

Potential wedlock with my girlfriend, the lovely Louise,

was right there for the taking. We'd sort of talked about boys'/ girls' night out and keeping in touch with our old friends, many of whom were still single. We'd sort the issues out best we could. Isn't that what marriage should be about? Shouldn't it be a learning experience? If I got married, my wife and I would pick the right time to have kids and then as parents get involved in their lives. We'd share the responsibility of basketball, ballet, or whatever. It would all work out just like it did with millions of other families.

> THEN I GOT TO THINKING ABOUT HOW MANY COUPLES HAD SPLIT UP AND WHY THEY'D BROKEN UP.

Then I got to thinking about how many couples had split up and why they'd broken up. Was it because they got tired of being together? Had they moved off in different directions? Or maybe, was it as simple as what Mr. B had described about the "top ten"?

I decided to ask several of my friends. Both older and younger. There are lots of couples who stay together and are not happy. They tend to live separate lives because they don't want to give up the money, status, and possessions they've amassed over the years.

Turns out most marriages that pass the test of time ascribe their happiness to Mr. B's theory. Those couples spend most of their time in each other's company doing things they both like. They hold hands a lot. They take vacations together. They belong to the same clubs. They golf and play bridge or gin rummy in groups. Could I see myself doing all those things with my lady? If we weren't on the same page now, how would it endure over time? Perhaps these "together things" blossomed as a marriage grew as both fell deeper and deeper in love.

Fast Eddie and I left Mr. B's place in a different state of mind. I went straight home, where I took out a bottle of Jamaican dark rum and a king-sized Coke and poured a shot into a canning jar filled with ice. Then, I headed for my favorite chair to reflect.

I had a decent job, but it wouldn't make me rich. What if I wanted to start a business, in Europe or New Zealand, or fight forest fires in Northern California? What if I wanted to work odd hours ... or work completely from home? What if I couldn't provide a lifestyle that was up to the level of her expectations? What if the path I chose didn't meet my wife's approval? Would she step up to the plate and give me the time and support I needed to succeed? What would happen to our relationship then? What would happen to our kids ... and our love for each other?

All sizzling-hot questions, and even after three drinks, I still didn't have a clue about the answers. Within two months, and multiple frank discussions, the force stepped in and altered my relationship's path. My lady and I stopped talking about marriage. We decided that without either of us having a concrete plan, especially me, there was no reason to step into the twilight zone. We decided to keep dating. If I still loved her in a couple of years when my shit was together, our supposed true love would blossom and marriage would always be available. I inwardly instructed Mr. T to take a break, so sex wouldn't cloud the issue.

Turns out, Mr. B's talk was prophetic. Mine and Fast Eddie's relationships lasted a couple more months. We both kinda-sorta split up, me first, then Ed a few weeks after that. Five minutes of Mr. B's insights rearranged my life. It got me to focus a little farther down the road, so when I proposed, I'd be able to have a better lifestyle, and ultimately, better balance. It also left me with a couple of burning questions. How, when, and where would I find those better things, and would either of my "top two" be around when I was ready? I could only hope.

I understood at that stage of my life that, thanks to our wonderful capitalistic society, everything you could ever want was out there. It was just a matter of who you met, when you met them, and who they were connected to. If you kept your eyes and ears open to what you were trying to find, it would appear.

This is the "Law of Intention." It states that if you intend to have something or someone, you must set the act in motion. If you work hard enough and pursue your goals with dedication, the stars will align and grant your wishes. Perhaps not in its entirety, but pretty close. And this definitely applies to marriage.

Unfortunately, most men get too preoccupied with their own ideas of marriage—or get side-tracked by Mr. T—and miss golden opportunities. Those are the ones who later in life say, "If only I had blah, blah, blah" or "My only regret in life is blah, blah, blah." You know these people. Maybe you're one of them, but you know that life is a great adventure, and you're usually exactly where you want to be.

***

The most singularly impressive feature of our culture (especially in the field of marriage) is that we have true freedom of choice. Our forefathers died in wars to guarantee this. Therefore, no matter where or who we end up with, we ulti-

> CHOICE IS THE
> MOST COLOSSAL
> INSTRUMENT IN
> FINDING BALANCE,
> AND IT'S THE ONLY
> WAY TO TRULY
> MANAGE MR. T.

mately have earned that ending. Choice is the most colossal instrument in finding balance, and it's the only way to truly manage Mr. T.

In marriage, or finding a partner, this is magnified. You have no one to blame but yourself. You choose your mate, and you gotta take the consequences. When the preacher says, "For better or for worse," most couples have selective hearing. That's why there are so many split-ups. When "worse" rears its ugly head, we're outta there. And that's a bit sad.

Choice is a difficult concept to swallow because it makes you responsible for your actions. Take the construction worker, for example. He grunts and bitches about working hard. All that manual labor but won't go back to school 'cause he's making money and parties hard. He's consumed by his testosterone and isn't disciplined enough to save, so he cannot get ahead. He knows he won't be able to pour cement or use a jackhammer all his life, but that's his choice—his consequences—to bear.

How about the teachers who complain about useless students and the politics of education? They're happy to take all that summer vacation while being locked into a cash cow, but they resent those who've stepped out into the business world and succeeded.

Marriage is no different. You take on the task, but what you do with it is totally up to you. Marriage takes work. And finding balance within the marriage takes way more work. But remember, each and every choice you make in that marriage has a consequence.

Start having social lunches with the secretarial pool and you and ole Mr. T will perk up. Have lunches with the upper management and see where that takes you. Drop your money at the casino or gamble online versus buying your wife chocolates, flowers, and jewelry. You'll reap what you sow.

Here's something for everyone who has made vows. Give and receive love unconditionally with no expectations. Carry a giant eraser around with you when you think about the past. If you do this, every day starts fresh, new, and potentially beautiful. This is what you should be looking for in a mate—someone who shares a vision for love and success. For without this duality and a passion to live in the moment, your selfishness will carve your relationship up like a turkey on Thanksgiving. Pass the stuffing, please!

Scoreboard: Marriage material

Testosterone: At the head of the class and very active while man hunts for his mate. Have no fear, Mr. T sticks his head out whenever and wherever woman congregate and is also willing to physically fight if necessary.

Balance: This is not a true scoring chapter either, but a reflective one on what could or could not be. Choice is monumental when it comes to balance. So it seems that one must keep "choice" in a truly sacred place. Hopefully, the good choices prevail, but there are many roadblocks and diversions ahead, enough to keep even the most focused male confused and frustrated. That's another bonus of having a hormone like T. But once he pulls the trigger and weds, he has a shot at fulfillment.

Score for this chapter: Another wash

Total: Out of balance: 3   In balance: 2

CHAPTER 12

THE BUSINESS OF BUSINESS

Get a job or start a business? Is Mr. T up for this challenge? He's supposed to be good for hunting. He's been in your hip pocket for the coed fornicating years. Now, maybe he'll go to bat for you with the savage assault you're about to lay on the corporate money-making machine.

Any bets on how long it'll be before I make my first million? In four years of undergrad work, or six for my master's, my studies pointed me to the same conclusion over and over. If I wasn't going to be a doctor or lawyer, from all the courses I took to the exams I wrote, I learned three keys words: "network, network, and network."

Today's workforce is full of nepotism. It's the same old story. If you live in a pit and surround yourself with cavemen, you'll end up in an artesian well treading water. If you read *The Wall Street Journal* or *The Globe and Mail* and brush shoulders with the financial district, chances are better you'll learn tricks about finances. No guarantees of course, but you are what you eat. If you spend your time on a surfboard, then you risk ending up as a beach bum or the inventor of the world's first solar-powered "rocket" board. It all depends on your approach and intelligence.

What happens if you have a rich daddy? Well, with a little luck and hard work, you're definitely at an advantage and half-way there.

"Dress for success," and all the other sayings aimed at life-style, are there for a reason. Practice what you preach and ye shall reap the rewards. This is the essence of business.

There are two approaches.

1. Link up with someone else's ideas and apply your knowledge and skill

2. Use your own idea and create a need for the product

THE NEED TO RISE UP AND MAKE SOMETHING OF YOURSELF IS ONE OF THE MOST PRIMAL URGES OF TODAY'S MAN.

The first idea is the status quo. You get hired by an existing company, and you either sell or service what that company offers. You get a paycheck in line with the level of your education or skills. You punch the clock and work your way up. The bigger the company, the more you need to network.

It really doesn't matter whether you're single, in a relationship, married with children, or living in a tent. The need to rise up and make something of yourself is one of the most primal urges of today's man. The pressure to attain is astronomical. So much so that the poor balancing scale gets tossed around literally from day to day as the poor boy tries to keep up with barrages of goodies flashed before him on every billboard, infomercial, and internet site.

From high fashion and high tech to the local health club, the need is great. And don't forget he's got to keep the little lady in luxury too, because she's seeing the same magnificent stuff out there.

It's a monstrous task that depresses Mr. T. The mission to achieve not only overwhelms our young hero but tosses him into the insatiable jaws of discontent and disappointment. This, of course, can lead to anger, drinking, doping, extramarital affairs, and the dark side. Unfortunately, these problems only increase the production of Mr. T. When you're talking conflict, that's where T shines, making the man rougher and tougher.

Finding the sweet spot in society without a lot of money weighs both our hero and heroine down. How does one try to keep up when they inherited all that money from Grandpa and Grandma? How about the ones who googled or "E-bay'd" themselves to the good life? Every infomercial brags of instant wealth, whether it's "NO MONEY DOWN" type real estate deals, trading tricks, or rapping your way to financial freedom on MTV.

These days, there seems to be a thousand ways to become rich. Everyone seems to be headed in the right direction, that is, everyone but you and most of your buddies. But the hill that leads to all the cash—you know, the "greener side"—has a hump you guys can't get over. Most of your crowd is barely making rent. And if there's any left over, it's often about buying into some basic luxury for your house or car.

If you've got babies, well, that's another story, 'cause diapers, strollers, car seats, and food cost a bundle. If there's anything left, you take your wife to a play, a concert, or a movie. Even going to the movies means dropping at least forty dollars. How the hell does anyone get ahead? So, for the masses, its Net Flicks or Hulu, that's the entertainment dollar maximized.

It turns out that nothing has really changed over the years. Hard work and a plan are the best ways to attain financial stability. Long-term wealth and ultimate freedom are attainable. The rules of society are more intact than ever. Supply and demand works in your job place and for your services, product, or consulting. It's still the best way to get ahead. Get some professional advice as soon as your paychecks exceed your living expenses, and save.

Put a percentage away each and every payday for special needs, rainy days, or a potential disaster. You'll save your marriage and your sanity, but you have to stick to the plan. It's about choices and self-discipline—keywords on the way to managing T and balance.

***

Making a living, whether you're a man or a woman, is one of the most important pulls and pushes on whether you can achieve peace. A reasonable amount of security goes a long way toward keeping the peace and satisfaction in life. And vice versa, the lack of security can put so much pressure on your relationship that it can crush the most potent love and eject you from the cockpit. So what to do?

First, take an interest in life and all its facets. Find motivating things and approach each day with pride and passion to achieve your goals, whether it's being a mechanic in a car shop, flipping burgers, working undercover, pumping gas, trading stocks and bonds, engineering skyscrapers, or becoming a professional.

Second, "adventurize" and revamp your current profession with a positive attitude. Look forward to each day and commit to the tasks assigned to you. If you approach your job (and life) like this, you will garner the respect and loyalty of your fellow employees and, more importantly, your employer (that's where advancement comes from).

Third, live by the basic rule that if you are happy, stay, but if the job becomes too rigid, tedious, or downright unpleasant, then leave. Don't worry too much about the consequences and your paycheck. One closed door always opens another, but you've got to be aware of the potential business openings that constantly surround you.

Fourth, have your eyes and ears open to opportunity. Granted, there may be a time when your particular job is not in tune with your best interests. Your responsibilities may make you tough it out for the "moola."

Fifth, and most important, you should never give up on getting what you want out of life—your dreams and a full diversified few decades on this planet. When you dream, you remain alive. If you have no dreams, you set a downward spiral in motion that can only lead to a bad and angry end.

When using these five principals, always remember the Law of Intention. Set a goal, and then put things in motion that can make it happen. And it's not always about material things. For instance, if you want people to treat you kindly, then you must make the effort to be friendly and courteous. If you're after a raise, then you must do something special to get it. If you want material things, make a list and start knocking things off one by one.

You can plan, save, and conquer, or you can spend, live fast
and loose, and suffer the outcome.
Remember, you always have a
choice, and you're exactly where
you put yourself. Good luck or
bad luck comes from preparation
or lack of one way or the other.

> GOOD LUCK OR BAD
> LUCK COMES FROM
> PREPARATION OR
> LACK OF ONE WAY
> OR THE OTHER.

Here's something to think about. You will have many disappointments in business, but misery after the fact is optional
and time consuming. So be aware that opportunity continually throws itself in your path and you can achieve whatever
you set out to do if you don't fixate on the failures.

***

I want to spend a few minutes discussing the duality of the
present-day businessman. The higher up the corporate ladder one gets, the more politically, socially, and sexually correct
one must be. Don't use Bill or Hilary Clinton here. They are
about as high as you can go corporately, but both were unable
to play down their indiscretions. *Remember, a blowjob is not
sex?* I can assure you that most men who get caught with their
unit in someone else's mouth don't get off so cleanly. Men in
Corporate America live with two or three distinct personalities depending on who the meeting is with.

Let's take a sidebar here. That's a pretty sad statement when
you think about it. Women tend to be themselves, speak their
minds, and give unedited opinions in the same corporate
locale. Why is that? Here's my opinion. Women complained
for decades that they were misunderstood, disrespected, used,
and abused. They ranted that men treated them like dirt, kept

them in their place, and so on. Granted, in the majority of cases, their complaints were warranted. Men were obtuse to most of their needs and maybe more. Watch a couple episodes of *Mad Men* (winner of a Golden Globe for best TV drama) and you'll see what I mean.

So what made it all change? Like it or not, got to give the bigger point to the boys. They listened hard and took the issues to heart. Then, they made the effort to correct the injustice. They knew it was the right thing to do and helped in every way possible to give those same women their reward, a path to equality!

Now, is it too much to ask women to allow us the same courtesy (namely, listen to how we feel and what is offensive to men)? Here's where we run into a brick wall!

Because we are basing our argument on emotions, we don't seem to be able to get our point across. Emotionally is the way women argue. They can't get their heads around debating emotions with men. They've had so much practice and excel at this approach that they dismiss our complaints like the wind.

Here's where the true feminists get more robust and shout from the highest mountain, "What the hell are you talking about, you sniveling lowlifes? You want us to listen to your complaints? Please, men have had it all since the beginning of time. We've just got here, and have only begun to feel the power and already you're complaining? You call yourself men? Let us enjoy ourselves before you try to take over like you've always done in the past. Okay?!"

Whoops! In other words, "Shut up!" we've been told, and there's not a lot we can do about it. Sound familiar, guys? Just like that, our testosterone shrivels, causing our jaws to lock shut. No retort possible. They win. It's like shooting fish in a barrel.

I want to return to the corporate boardroom, where men are still mostly in charge. Let me give you a couple of examples on how current bosses deal with running the show. If you're a CEO, or in any position of authority in a meeting, you must have your speech proofread a few times so you don't say anything that may compromise your integrity or offend any of your shareholders. You must be sensitive to color, race, creed, and religion. No big deal here, it's just good business practice and respect for all.

> I'M SAYING TRUTH IS A FLEETING WINDOW WITH OPAQUE GLASS THESE DAYS, ISN'T IT?

Once the meeting is over, you meet with your handpicked team to discuss the outcome. There you can speak more freely, but still must watch your Ps and Qs. Once that meeting is over, you review the results with your two most trusted coworkers. Then and only then can you use the words and context you really mean. Mincing words and rhetoric are all too familiar in today's business and political arenas. I'm not saying it's the wrong approach; I'm saying truth is a fleeting window with opaque glass these days, isn't it? Of course, it doesn't stop at the top. Every level of employment must comply.

***

Let's look at an everyday Joe, who works in the parts department for a major auto company. He's surrounded by mostly men. On the job, in the back room, he can be pretty frank about his work. Once he gets up to the counter, depending on the client, his vernacular changes. How he deals with his suppliers and clients is also subject to interpretation because of who's on the other end of the phone.

When both the CEO and parts guys get home, they will unwind. Some may greet their wives with a hug and a kiss, talk to their kids, or grab a beer or stronger. Some might need to be alone. But each and every man must find a way to control the frustration and problems he faces day to day. This is the balancing act we all face.

Work and play is a challenge for both testosterone and balance. Men must constantly be aware of their surroundings and what they can and cannot say in our society. I guess that's progress, but wouldn't it be cool in business if sometimes we could blurt out what's on our minds without having to justify or be scrutinized for saying it? To us, it seems like women can do this quite freely these days.

So where is old T in a biz relationship? Well, it depends on the gender and position of his coworking team. If the "old boys' club" is running the show, our hero can rule with traditional machismo and a dash of equality, but if the majority of the gang is female, or the HR person is in on the deal, then T is subjected to the proverbial "watch what you say and how you say it" syndrome.

Lord forbid, he works under a women's rule, where he has to hide in corners to breathe. Aha. Caught you, didn't I? See how quickly you judged that sentence to be sexist? Shit hits the fan in a nanosecond when we step out of line. These are the realities of the modern workplace. Women definitely have the upper hand while men are x-rayed and get an oral exam every time they open their mouth. So, boys, may the bird of paradise do the backstroke in your corporate goulash! Good luck and hang in there, buddy!

Scoreboard: The business of business

Testosterone: In business, Testy is definitely a factor. You must regulate the flow in order to be successful.

Balance: This is another wash chapter, as balance is completely dependent on personal growth, the percentage of females you deal with, and expectations versus corporate posturing and self-esteem.

Score for this chapter: One more wash

Total: Out of balance: 3   In balance: 2

CHAPTER 13

CHILDREN OR NOT, HERE I COME

Children make you happier than you've ever been, and at the same time try your patience more than you could ever imagine. Yet, isn't procreation the purpose of living? I mean, isn't it the duty of every human being to perpetuate the race and keep the bloodline going?

At some point in time, all men feel the need to nurture, protect, and shield loved ones from harm. We also need to share experiences and pass our wisdom down to the next generation. Hence, we desire a mate, father offspring, and then protect the flock. It's nature.

Where do children fit into man's personal equation of balance? What choice do you have? Once they're out of the womb, screaming and gulping down oxygen, demanding designer jeans and the keys to your Porsche, you don't have many options. You've initiated life (a good example of the

"Law of Intention") and now you're stuck with the results. We're not debating whether or not we should bring children into the world; we're just gauging what effect those little rug rats have on T and balance.

Being a proud father is also a rite that every man should have the option to enjoy. There's nothing like parental ownership and pride when your little guy or girl shines in the classroom, on the playing field, in the school choir, or in any other endeavor. You relish all the firsts, the first discernible word (especially if it's "dada"), first tooth, first step, first kiss, first time on a bicycle, first catch with a baseball glove, and so on.

> BEING A PROUD FATHER IS ALSO A RITE THAT EVERY MAN SHOULD HAVE THE OPTION TO ENJOY.

But what about the flip side of the coin? The first "no," temper tantrum, or "I hate you"? Then there's the first time they ask you to leave them alone, their first curse word, or first time they get caught drinking. The list goes on, but you get the point. This second list is as painful as the first is euphoric.

Would you trade any of the good or bad experiences? Of course not. They all will happen. And of course, the number of children only compounds the issues and spreads the stress and joy over the years, which fly by. During the child-rearing years, there are so many things going on in our hero's world that by the time he's in his forties or fifties, he can barely remember what went on.

Remember back when you were a kid? You played with toys and spent a lot of time outside with other kids. You played hopscotch, hide and seek, marbles, tennis, baseball, touch football, and so on. Were you one of those kids that only came home to eat or sleep? Computers hadn't been invented yet, and TV wasn't that big a deal. Maybe you watched Ed Sullivan, *Leave It to Beaver*, Walt Disney, and *The Jetsons*. If you're a little younger, maybe you were into *Star Trek*, *Dallas*, Maxwell Smart, or some of the other evening soaps. Maybe you even watched that stuff with your folks.

My point is that parents in the twenty-first century have no clue as to what our kids are doing with technology, and they have a hard time sharing the experience. Case in point. I remember thinking I was the bomb when I was in Japan and picked up one of the first Walkmans—you know, that handheld tape recorder you could carry around and wear earphones with. I mean, that was state of the art, and when I brought it home, everyone wanted to see how it worked and hear how it sounded. It wasn't difficult for my parents to figure it out. It was a tape recorder, smaller and cute, but they understood it.

Today's kid grow up with the internet, cell phones, iPods, Blackberrys, reality shows, YouTube, Facebook, Twitter, Instagram and the list is never ending. They even have free access to Porn and many right and left wing radical sites where propaganda is livid. Where does that put us as parents? What does it do to Mr. T and balance? Our kids know more about technology than we do, and yet we're trying to tell them what's right and wrong. Let's be real. We are, for the most part, tech stupid and quite frankly at our age happy to be out of the loop. However, being ignorant is not a good place to preach from, so we must try to at least understand what our kids are doing with their time.

***

Let's review the husband's situation. He's got kids and has to support them. He has to manage his time within every aspect of his marriage. He deals with work, kids, friends, socializing, money in, money out, sleeping, eating, shopping, getting things fixed, looking for furniture, barbecuing, and watching the occasional sporting event. And if there is any time or energy left, he might be lucky enough to catch his wife in a sensuous mood and make love.

> AND IF THERE IS ANY TIME OR ENERGY LEFT, HE MIGHT BE LUCKY ENOUGH TO CATCH HIS WIFE IN A SENSUOUS MOOD AND MAKE LOVE.

Wow! How far he's come since the days of seed spreading. Our once frenetic, sex-crazed boy has turned into a pretty docile guy who has massive doses of duty and expectations heaped on his shoulders. Pillage and plunder are worlds away and have passed through the exit signs a long time ago.

His state of heightened sexual desires has been put on the back burner while he sashays through his mad, mad, mad, world. Let's not forget that men in general are still thinking about sex every few seconds even as they age, so where does that leave him?

Well, we're civilized, right? We have to accept reality. There's more to life than sex. (Oh, really? Still coming to grips with the truth, are we?) After a few years of marriage and kids, there's no way we can come home and expect to fulfill our need for lust, is there? It's bad enough we talk about it, think about it, and joke about it on a regular basis with our buddies, who are pretty much in the same boat: a downward-spiraling, dwindling state of sexual activity.

By the way, whatever happened to the days when you and

your wife couldn't keep your hands off each other? I think that was before the wedding, and maybe for a while after, but then the kids come along and *zap*, presto, change-o, suddenly sex is a luxury, like a Hawaiian vacation. Should I dare say, and just about as often?

Okay, take it easy! I can hear women yelling at me, "*You* spend nine months with something growing inside of you, give birth, and then see how fast you want to have sex again!"

Ouch.

Most women really know how to deflate a man's ego and erection. They don't do it with intended malice, but being repeatedly told, "No, not tonight" or "Maybe tomorrow night." And yes, of course, we understand the tremendous burden and demands that pregnancy puts on our mate.

> MOST WOMEN REALLY KNOW HOW TO DEFLATE A MAN'S EGO AND ERECTION.

However, that's a lie. We really don't. Just as a woman can never feel the pain of what it's like to get kicked in the nuts, men can never feel what goes on during a pregnancy or what giving birth does to your partner.

We can only hypothesize and try to compensate by being compassionate. We can only assume what the nine-month term must feel like without a hope in hell of ever walking in their shoes. That's the way it's supposed to be. I'm a man. I do not have the ability to get pregnant.

***

Having kids is like trying to catch a minnow in a pond while you are blindfolded. Fact is, it's impossible! Can our hero be in balance during these merry-go-round years? The crises and demands are so diverse and so personal it's amazing if you last long enough to see your kids grow up. Once that day arrives, you will have a chance to come up for air and reexamine where the testosterone in your life has been hiding.

In my parents' day, there seemed to be some of the population who had a simple, straightforward life, and those people seemed content. But in my generation and all the people I know, this is not the case. There is considerable discontent out there. I can't really think of one family or couple who hasn't gone through difficult times. The ones who are standing the test of time have issues like we all do. Ultimately, who knows what the truth is?

It doesn't seem to matter whether people have a little or a vault full of money, they are still struggling to find a piece of the puzzle that's missing. They mull it over at dinner parties. They search for it at social gatherings and PTA meetings. They all want to know where to look to find what's missing. Is the answer a long walk along the sandy shore of a faraway secluded beach? You may find some peace there, but is it enough?

> IT DOESN'T SEEM TO MATTER WHETHER PEOPLE HAVE A LITTLE OR A VAULT FULL OF MONEY, THEY ARE STILL STRUGGLING TO FIND A PIECE OF THE PUZZLE THAT'S MISSING.

Can money buy cerebral peace? Maybe not, but it can certainly get you booked first class on that secluded beach on a private island! However, that is only physical peace, so the answer is still no. Money can buy security, lawn service, house cleaning, cars, jewelry, and houses, but peace can only come from inside of you. Kids can help bring you a parental peace if you spend the time getting to know them.

Perhaps your dose of that elusive peace comes after they leave the nest. Stay strong, you will get your chance. No doubt kids cause chaos, for good and for bad. They cause joy and pain. They push you to the limits of the farthest galaxies. But the one indisputable thing they force upon you is to be in balance. Because if you lose it around them, then your world explodes and there is much, much less hope for peace anytime soon.

Scoreboard: "Children or Not, Here I Come"

Testosterone: Who has time to think about Mr. T? I'm way too busy. I know he's there 'cause I get a rush when I see a pretty girl, but hands off. Once I have kids, Testy is confined to my job and my current state of frustration and anger.

Balance: We admit our hero experiences glimpses of balance even though there's so much crap to deal with. But he's juggling work, the kids, the wife, and the bills, trying not to break. We're going to be lenient, 'cause if he's made it to this point, he's becoming a well-rounded dad. Great job, Pops. Giving you props on this chapter.

Score for this chapter: Balance to some degree, let's give him 0.5.

Total: Out of balance: 3   In balance: 2.5

**After forty or fifty years of slugging it out, after his kids have grown up, our hero is close to hitting .500 in the balance department. Is that a coincidence considering that age coincides with a marked decrease of Mr. T flowing through his system? I'll let you be the judge. But don't make any assumptions until you read the next chapter. We can rehash the whole thing then.

CHAPTER 14

MIDLIFE CRISIS: THE EBBING OF MR. T

The last kid has finally left the nest. The economy is tough, but I'm doing pretty well. Things are settling down, and for the first time in years, I have time on my hands. Now what?

I should take up a hobby again, but I can't remember what I like doing. I'm too old to play competitive sports, unless it's squash or some light tennis. I could take up golf. I'm still too young for shuffleboard, right?

Suddenly, I begin to notice that there's a lot going on out there. There's ski clubs, social clubs, dance-a-thons, and charity walks. There are lots of people doing lots of things. I've been boarded up with my wife, working my job and raising kids for so long that I've missed it all. Other than dinner parties, office socials, and following our kids around, there was no time to get involved with outside interests.

Over the last decade, the internet has spawned all kinds of

sites for the active lifestyle. My wife and I are still together, but she has changed. We both have changed, that's for sure. I guess I still love her, but maybe it's more like we tolerate each other.

I'm starting to see a lot of young chicks who look pretty good, and a lot of them are looking back at me. Why do young women want to tease older married guys? I'm flattered and, I admit, tempted. That can only mean one thing. Mr. T is back. I can feel it.

WHY DO YOUNG WOMEN WANT TO TEASE OLDER MARRIED GUYS?

Because of my childless new-found freedom, I think I'll do some upgrading, and I'm going to be selfish. Through the years I've sacrificed a lot. I'm going to buy some cool threads, shoes, a new stereo with wireless speakers, and maybe even a new car. Something fast and low to the ground. As a matter of fact, I think I'll spoil myself by grabbing that "U-Boat" sports watch with the rubber wristband I've been eyeing for three years. Might as well indulge myself with that too.

I'm going to spend some cash on these old bones. After all these years of taking care of everyone else, I deserve it. I think I'll start to work out on a regular basis, join a fitness club, and maybe try yoga. I'm going to get out there and live again. Are you ready for me world? Here I come. Drum roll, please.

CAN MAN SURVIVE THE MIDLIFE CRISIS?

"Midlife crisis" (MLC for short) is a term that became popular in the sixties. That's when everything was up for grabs: power, sex, money, love, freedom, drugs, and rebellion. Those years had it all, and as the aging population saw an opportunity to get back its youth, it spared no expense.

It really didn't matter whether you were poor or if you had millions, you saw yourself getting old. You witnessed all those young people having fun and decided you needed to retrofit yourself. That spawned a multitrillion-dollar business of refitting, rewiring, relifting, and regretting.

Suddenly, plastic surgeons came out of the woodwork like mice to a cheese party, all of them claiming they could perform miracles. They could lift your face, cheeks, ass, and eyes. Most of all, they could lift your checkbook without laying a finger on it. Utopia wasn't too far around the corner either. You could cheat Father Time, prolong your desires, and even maintain youthful levels of testosterone.

Voila! Old guys (forty and up) were leaving their wives and driving red Corvette convertibles faster than GM could crank 'em out. Those ragtops were laden with pubescent babes in bikinis strewn across their bucket seats. California hedonism ranked at the top of the list for this kind of behavior, and it drove men crazy.

Why grow old with your wife, with her declining body and looks, when you could convince yourself you were still a stud. We really weren't paying much attention to the fact that our biceps were flopping around, our pecs had disappeared, and our gut was hanging over our belts. It didn't matter! You were top management, or at least well established, and could attract the hot young babes.

Your pals slap you on the back, telling you how great it must feel to have such a beautiful young babe, but you know the truth. You're falling asleep around nine or ten watching television. Meanwhile, your "newfound love" (this is sarcasm) would rather be out dancing at a club with people who can actually dance.

You keep the charade going for a while, and then you

might move on to another hot young chick, depending on the thickness of your bankroll. Some things are true whether you accept them or not. You are an old fart. Sure, Viagra can keep you in the game … for a while. You might even fool yourself into believing the hottie really wants you, but the thought has crossed your mind that she might be using you. After all, you have the money and position to further her status.

> DO YOU REALLY WANT TO SPEND THE NEXT DECADE WITH SOMEONE TWENTY OR THIRTY YEARS YOUNGER?

So come on, can it last? Does it have any meaning? Do you really want to spend the next decade with someone twenty or thirty years younger? Imagine those later years, suffering while she changes your diapers. The poor girl is in the prime of her life. Come on! Stop being so egotistical, feeling sorry for yourself. Get a grip. We were meant to be with partners similar in age. We were meant to share life, not teach it or wait for it to catch up.

I know the whole sugar daddy thing is seductively attractive, but it fails 99.99 percent of the time. If you think you are the 0.01 percent that does end up with a hot young chick, in ten years it won't matter because she won't be so hot, and you'll be even older. Drop me a line if it ain't so.

***

MLC is totally misunderstood. It's not about trying to be young again, which is impossible. Youth and the way you manage your life comes from inside your brain. You are as young as you think. That doesn't mean you can physically run the hundred-meter dash in under ten seconds when you're forty or fifty. It means that you can have an articulate free mind that allows you to cherish the moment and still dream.

That's what we have as kids, and that's what youth is all about. The ability to have fun, not judge, to create and take pleasure in the things we like. Kids don't have emotional baggage to stop them from living life. All the shit rolls off their backs like rainwater off a duck. Kids just want to have fun. Shouldn't we want the same thing as we age? Isn't this the secret of dying happy? As a matter of fact, I'm certain it is. It's the decrease in testosterone that allows us to finally get there.

> IT'S THE DECREASE IN TESTOSTERONE THAT ALLOWS US TO FINALLY GET THERE.

One man, who had re-wed at sixty, blamed his previous fifty years, and two failed marriages, on Mr. T. He openly confessed to his ex-wives (five years after the fact) that Mr. T had made him so sex crazed he couldn't think straight. But at sixty, with his new wife and much lower levels of T, he was finally able to think rationally and enjoy life for what it is.

Do differences in testosterone separate youth's aggressive nature from the staunch, grouchy, bigoted, cranky, unforgiving, pissed off, deceived, scarred, and generally miserable portion of the older male population? Of course it does. Wait a minute. There's no mention of happiness in either camp. Are men happy at any time in their lives? Is this the reason men spiral helplessly out of control and enter the weightless time capsule of the MLC?

Let's take a poll of ten men who are in MLC. Hands up, guys. How many of you are happy when you meet an interesting woman? How many stay happy with her if she's not putting out? How many of you are happy when you score with a gorgeous woman, even if it doesn't last that long? How many are happy with your current wife? How many are happy when they receive a promotion? Were you happy bringing up your kids? How many of you were happy when you achieved financial independence? If your wife makes more than you, does that make you happy? How happy are you taking orders from your female boss? Do you get to spend enough time with your buddies? Have you fulfilled any of your dreams? Are you happy when you wake up in the morning? If you put your hand up eight or more times, you're a happy man.

Most middle-aged men are lucky to get past six. I'm referring to the ones who've had a couple of decades of getting beaten up. There's a lot of rage out there—and from both sexes. Inherently, all people would prefer to be nice, kind, understanding, and loyal, yet in day-to-day social interaction we are inundated with complaints about everything. It's a quagmire of dissatisfaction with jobs, governments, fear, world issues, stock markets, health care, and disease.

> WE ARE SO LIMITED BY OUR OWN RULES THAT WE'VE FORGOTTEN WHAT IT'S LIKE TO BE HAPPY AND FREE.

Society puts a tremendous amount of limitations on us. The rules stipulate our parameters, from how many garbage bags you can put out on your driveway to where you can or cannot smoke. It also dictates who can belong to the ultra-rich clubs we realize we will never be allowed to join. The list is never ending. We are so limited by our own rules that we've forgotten what it's like to be happy and free. Quite a paradox in a free society, yes?

Who do we look to for help in midlife? Where can we find answers? I'm not going to give one cent of my hard-earned money to a shrink, because they're more screwed up than most of us. Plus, they want to charge us to feed their habit. Yeah, I don't think so. The question remains, Where do we go?

> I HAVE THOUGHT LONG AND HARD ABOUT THIS, AND HERE'S WHAT I'VE COME UP WITH.

I have thought long and hard about this, and here's what I've come up with. Every macho, chauvinistic asshole who has ever roamed the planet in search of food, shelter, a mate, a family, a job, a war, salvation, or any purpose always ends up wanting the same thing: to be in a tranquil place and to be loved. No matter how much testosterone flows through his body, especially during MLC, his true goal is to be with someone he loves and who loves him in return.

Love makes the world go round. This is one truth that cannot be denied. Men who don't find love refute this, but deep down inside they know they're lying. They spew all kinds of bs about how they don't give a buffalo chip about love, and they treat women as sexual outlets. They exert their physical power over those same women and tell them to be seen and not heard.

If you could look inside every man, you'd find that the search for love is indelibly etched into his soul. Man dreams to be loved and is a pussycat once he finds it. Right from the time his momma pulls him to her breast until he marries the woman of his dreams, he searches for love until his dying breath. If he doesn't find it, or is spurned, he becomes angry and sullen and will revert to rape, pillage, and plunder.

I mean, if you're not in love, you need to take your frustrations out on someone or something. That's Mr. T's mission. If I'm not getting my share of love, why should anyone be happy? It's that simple!

***

"What are you thinking right now?" comes back to my mind. Is this question related to the MLC? Let's backtrack. Thirty years ago, when a woman asked me that question, I freaked out and nearly scratched my head until a bald spot occurred. Now that I've suffered through a significant portion of my life, the answer is as clear as a bell. Before I tell you what that answer is, let's examine why it comes so swiftly and succinctly at a mature age. How can MLC be defeated? Let me review the stages man has endured.

I'm sure you've been through a lot. We all have. We've lusted, loved, married, had kids, dealt with many jobs, made mistakes, and had one or two home runs. In my time here, I've learned one thing: Only you, and you alone, can take care of yourself. Your wife, your kids, your relatives, your friends, and your coworkers depend on you, but when it comes right down to it, you are the only one who can shape your existence. Granted, if you have a great woman at your side who supports you, you'll have a better chance, but ultimately it rests on your shoulders. MLC is a state of mind, and it's all about choice.

Every choice you've made put you on some kind of path. While you were on that path, you made some good picks, a few mediocre ones, and some that were simply awful. This brings us back to the "Law of Intention." Because now when I reflect, I can see what my intentions were before they began. Twenty-twenty hindsight proves to me that where I am today is exactly where I put myself. This is the preamble to my answer for the "What am I thinking right now?" question.

The answer is a revelation, a breakthrough moment in my midlife. It puts MLC into logical terms that a man can grasp. Open your mind and let the following ideas rattle around in your brain before you make a quick judgment or form an opinion. In other words, be receptive. Find a place where you can be alone. Take a deep breath and read the next italicized paragraphs a couple of times OUT LOUD. Then, decide how they apply to you, especially if you are in MLC. Here we go. This is my take on defeating MLC.

I'm absolutely certain that I am exactly where I'm supposed to be at this exact moment. Every event, every preference, and every consequence that came from the choices I made has brought me to where I am. I am the culmination of all that has passed. And you know what? I am at complete and total peace with this assessment.

> THIS IS THE KEY TO DEFEAT MLC: SURRENDER TO WHO AND WHAT YOU ARE. IF A MAN DOES THAT, HE HAS NO CHOICE BUT TO ACCEPT AND LOVE HIMSELF.

This is the key to defeat MLC: surrender to who and what you are. If a man does that, he has no choice but to accept and love himself.

So after giving in to this realization, I am for the first time in a long time totally in balance, and my testosterone is neutral.

I'm not happy, sad, frustrated, or anything else. I am content. Praise be to Allah, the Lord, the Force, Buddha, and the Dali Lama. God is great! But I really don't care. I realize the reason I feel happy and finally at peace is because I've been liberated from my deeds, and I am free to think about or do anything I want. My past is irrelevant.

Here's the leap of faith and the answer:

I decree that my future will be a positive revelation and an adventure. I make this conscious decision right now. I'm going to go forward from here and find a place that gives me freedom and peace. To get there I need to be in balance, and the plan must include love. This is the answer to "What are you thinking right now?"

I'm searching and searching. I'm digging deeper, and I think I feel the answer coming. It's almost here, and I can nearly make it out. I feel my body starting to tingle, and it's got nothing to do with T.

Here it is. Holy Moly! It's been here the whole time! The reason I'm in a midlife crisis is because of LOVE, or more precisely, the LACK of love.

I know I'm spot on with this observation. Midlife crisis is, by definition, a predicament where one is not getting what they think they deserve, especially love. Let me think about that for a second. Way back, when I got married, I remember feeling loved, but what's more important is the feeling of love I was putting out. I mean, there was no mountain high enough, no valley low enough, no river wide enough, right? We've all sang that song. Being in love was unbelievable, undeniable, and ultra-cosmic. Where, oh where has my little love affair gone?

The little voice inside my head just shouted the words "focus on balance." Right! It's telling me that this crisis—this "love I deserve"—is one sided. The opposite of "love I deserve" is the "love I need to give." Have I told anyone lately that I loved them and meant it? When I greet my wife, are my kisses on her cheeks or the peck on her lips meaningful? Honestly, I'm lacking in the whole "love" thing. This is what has led to boredom and MLC. It's a self-inflicted, personal disaster.

This empty, hollow feeling that is causing my midlife calamity is easily identifiable as the absence of love. It's for the love of me and the world around me. It's about loving what is available to me. You don't need to be a brain surgeon to get traction here. It's not selfish love, the kind that puts my needs in front of everything; it's love for everything around me.

Birds, nature, trees, the ocean, my eyesight, my taste buds, the home I live in, the shoes I put on my feet, my two cats, my wife, our children, each and every breath I inhale and exhale, even the computer and keyboard that I'm banging on right now. I got caught up in the hunt for Material Supremacy and have taken the miracle of life's awesomeness for granted. I want to fall in love with life again. I want to regain the childish perspective of the wonderment of life and dreams. Will a younger woman bring that to me? I don't think so. The changes have to come from within.

What am I thinking right now? I'm thinking about moving to a state of mind that comes from loving all that's around me. When you're "in love," nothing can break this spell. We talked about how young love can make us all crazy, but realizing how to give and receive love is much more powerful. It comes with years and years of the trials and tribulations of a challenging life. Isn't the pursuit of love what everyone is after? Isn't this why fairy tales, books, songs, poems, sonnets, fantasies, and hope are all about?

Receiving love is divine creation's most sought-after goal. When you're a child, you do everything you can to get acceptance from your parents and friends. You want to receive their love, so you do things that will reward you with this goal. There's no midlife crisis when you're young because love is flowing and you haven't had the time to discard it. You also haven't had time to feel life's pains that tend to obliterate Love.

Later in life, men buy flowers for women and give gifts like jewelry and other items that are a total waste of money. It's because they want to show their love and receive love back.

Young love doesn't need those kinds of tokens. Along with hugs, kisses, and lovemaking, it's the immaterial things that count. A certain look, thought, or gesture are all unconditional ways of showing love. As we get older, our need to please the people we love becomes murky.

How does one express love when we can't use sex as the tool or testosterone as an excuse? We want to be genuine, thus we offer ourselves freely to show our love. Instead of flowers and gifts, we want to give our love, our kindness, our sympathy, our compassion for all around us, especially those who have less. This is how we attain peace, satisfaction, and balance. This is the only way to defeat the midlife blues. Do it through words and actions.

HAVE YOU READ THIS A COUPLE OF TIMES AND ALLOWED IT TO SINK IN?

Have you read this a couple of times and allowed it to sink in? Good. Because, this is the crux of the crisis. There are two types of love: physical and mental. Both are alive and vacillating within every relationship at all times. In the beginning, things are skewed so that a high percentage is physical, and a lower amount of mental love. It evens out once the sex cools off, and then toward the end it's mostly mental.

It's during the transformation that MLC may rear its ugly head, because we've forgotten how to give and receive love. And because of that, we are damn well going to find it any way we can and with anyone who'll give it to us. But it's a false sense of secure love and only makes us worse for wear.

I'm guessing here, but it's a pretty good bet, that the majority of males who don't experience a midlife crisis find the transition from physical to mental love seamless. There is no rapid drop off of physical love, and what is lost is immediately gobbled up on the mental side. There is no need to go on the hunt for a newer, younger version of what you think you have lost.

But "lost love" is not the only area we seek when trying to overpower the randomness of a midlife crisis. We also are on the hunt for truth. Remember a few pages back when our hero first heard voices about what to do, or not do, and if it was good or bad? Well, that voice for many is muted through the volatile years of getting established and parenting.

As we age, that voice (you might want to use conscience or intuition here) starts to make inroads. If you are alone or in a quiet place, close your eyes right now and pull back from what you're reading. Wait a few minutes and you will start to hear thoughts. It may be confusing at first, but if you initiate a conversation inside your head, you may be surprised at what happens. If you can't do this right now, make the time to do it later, but do it. It's different for everyone, but it's there.

> IT MAY BE CONFUSING AT FIRST, BUT IF YOU INITIATE A CONVERSATION INSIDE YOUR HEAD, YOU MAY BE SURPRISED AT WHAT HAPPENS.

It's a connection to, I don't know, another planet, another world, another you in a parallel universe? Call it what you will, it's real, and as we get older, we should attune to it more and more. You'll find with a little practice that you can have intimate and truthful conversations with this voice. It will advise you. It's not the same as crazy people talking to themselves; it's actually quite the opposite.

It's a means of self-direction.

For example, if you make a little movie inside your head about stealing money from a little old lady, your inner voice will be telling you that's not very kosher. A simple example, but you get the drift.

Maybe the voice is from your next, or past, lifetime. It's aiming you in a direction to complete your earthly task in this lifetime. Whatever the source of the voice may be, why not ask yourself some pointed questions about your current situation and see what the voice has to say? You've got nothing to lose.

You know for sure that you are right here, right now and the choices you've made are done. It's only future choices that will shape the rest of your days until you die. After all, without any conscious theories about life, you would only be walking warmth. I'm certain you're much more.

So how do you get yourself out of MLC? Surely, you'd like to spend your best years when you are healthy and vibrant in a state of happiness and balance and avoid this type of catastrophe. How can you do that without spending thousands of dollars on health, plastic surgery, or chiropractic care?

> BE CONSISTENT.
> MAKE THE
> EFFORT.

I say the best way is to wake up every morning with positive energy in your heart. Greet your wife or the first person you see with a loving touch, kiss, or encouraging word and see what the response is. Be consistent. Make the effort. Leave your home with a smile and positive attitude. Do this and see how the world responds to you. Nobody is going to sit here and tell you that everything will come up roses, but living in this way is putting into action the Law of Intention.

You want a better world, and a better life for yourself? Do

you want to kick the MLC blues? Then you must start the ball rolling. No matter how badly the world has treated you, you can change your life by offering love, or at least a happier version of yourself. You cannot feel sorry for yourself if you've been disappointed a thousand times, if you've lost your job, your girlfriend, wife, family, 401K, or most of your possessions.

You need to realize that every waking moment, every breath you take, every second that ticks by on the clock is a chance at a new beginning. It's completely and totally up to you. You are in charge of your life and the limitations you put on yourself are, only because you put them there. It's like the only thing we fear is fear itself. Of course, this has nothing to do with where your testosterone is going, but it does have to do with taking charge of a balanced life.

> YOU NEED TO REALIZE THAT EVERY WAKING MOMENT, EVERY BREATH YOU TAKE, EVERY SECOND THAT TICKS BY ON THE CLOCK IS A CHANCE AT A NEW BEGINNING.

Be committed to this positive behavior and watch the crisis you once saw through dark-colored glasses starting to brighten up with sunshine. Your world will recharge itself through the love and positive energy you're putting out, because, if you drop a pebble in still water, the waves will eventually reach every corner of the pond. That's what happens when you set something in motion. It's the "Law of Cause and Effect."

Think about it. You can see, feel, touch, taste, and smell. You live in a country that has unlimited potential for those who are willing to risk and believe in their dreams. Why don't most people reach their dreams? Because they stop trying or they get sidetracked with the brutality of The Hunt for Material Supremacy (i.e., real life). Once again, I reiterate. *Disappointment is a reality; misery after the fact is an option.*

In midlife, perhaps it's too late to achieve the dreams we had as children or young adults, but opportunity is still there in ways that are much more important than material gains, fame, or fortune. I can guarantee that most fifty- to sixty-year-old men would choose a loving family and good health over humungous wealth and heart disease. What's the point of killing yourself for all that money only to leave it to the ones you didn't spend time loving?

So we've come to the end of the "Midlife Crisis" chapter, and we've seen how it can be dealt with. And what have we discovered?

1. What's the point of trying to relive your youth once it's over? It's pointless.

2. Now that I have more time on my hands, I need to get back in love with life. It starts with loving myself, then I can spread that love to those around me.

3. I want to have peace as I grow into my twilight years.

4. I need to reestablish a connection with my own identity through the voices in my head.

5. I can change my life and all around me any second, any minute of any day.

6. I realize love and a positive attitude is the answer to finding balance and the cure to MLC.

These bullet points are not something males would usually take to heart—there's way too much emphasis on love, peace, and girlie emotional mishmash. But man is, like we said, pretty much a blunt object, and this softer part of him must be pounded in for him to get the message.

So it seems that after T dwindles, we can finally see that the spoils of war, strife, and hunting for material gain mean squat. Those extra thirty or so years of "non-childbearing" life expectancies need to be fulfilling. When T's traits diminish, it opens our eyes and hearts to love. Almost every soldier who is dying in the field, every cancer patient on their death bed, or every heart attack victim uses the word "love" aimed at someone just before the end.

My case rests.

So what are you waiting for? Get rid of MLC. Get back in love with life.

Scoreboard: Midlife crisis

Testosterone: The hunt is pretty much over. You've amassed and screwed your way to your current position, and no amount of T will change that.

Balance: If you've hit the wall in your personal life and can't cope, then you've reached midlife crisis and you are really out to lunch and balance. If you can relearn how to love, we'll give one point to each category.

Score for this chapter: One in and one out.

Total: Out of balance: 4   In balance: 3.5

**Well, here we are again. So what do you think? Balance, out of balance? It can be frustrating. We live longer than any other time in history, and we have a whole new set of rules and standards to hit. Our relationships are pulled and pushed like never before, but we know Mr. T is causing less havoc 'cause we struggle less with control and power. Men are burnt out and just hanging in there, surfing the sports channels trying to find solace and happiness.

Women, however, are hitting their midlife crisis at sixty and discovering there is a whole new world out there for them. They are traveling with their girlfriends, seeking new jobs and experiences, joining social clubs, going to spas and yoga lessons, going on wine tasting, boat cruises and bicycle tours in Tuscany, walking the Great Wall of China—wanting to live. It's like playing Snakes and Ladders. Once again, we're as different as night and day.

CHAPTER 15

MORE LOVE, MORE RELATIONSHIPS

We've stumbled past midlife, and as men we've made some discoveries. We're not as physically strong as we thought we were ... or as demanding. We need less food and sex. We've backed off on the hunt for material supremacy and the need to be in command. We're happy to let younger people do things for us.

We've had our biyearly checkup. Our blood pressure, cholesterol, triglycerides, and white blood cell counts are all within tolerance. We've got the thumbs-up on the colonoscopy, angiogram, and prostate procedures. We've hit fifty, which is the new forty, or maybe we've hit sixty, which is the new fifty.

Congratulations. We're in good shape, except for the wrinkles, crow's feet, chicken necks, and age spots. But screw all that—it only makes us more distinguished. Ask anyone, especially the women. What now? Has all the testosterone in our system been used up? Are we preparing for the end?

***

Mortality creeps into our thoughts, as most of us have witnessed friends and family who have moved on to the next world. But you're not there yet, and by any standards there's a lot left in the tank. Each day is a chance to have one more great day. And that's the way you should see it. When you wake up in the morning or from an afternoon nap—that's right, a nap (you can use the rest, just like toddlers do)—you should greet the day with a smile. You see the sunshine and feel its warmth, then stick your face into the cool wind or feel the rain skittering off your head as it rolls off the stubble on your chin. It's all a marvel to be alive, to sense things—how great that still is!

> IT'S ALL A MARVEL TO BE ALIVE, TO SENSE THINGS— HOW GREAT THAT STILL IS!

In the movie *City of Angels,* Nicolas Cage plays an angel from above who asks Meg Ryan, a real human, "What does a pear taste like, to you?" She must describe the sweet, grainy texture to the angel. As time continues, he becomes tortured by not being able to experience her in "the flesh." So because of his love for her, he gives up his perfect existence and falls from heaven to become human. Now he experiences pain, bleeding, a hot shower, food, and the ability to breathe and to make love. For him, it's the ultimate experience, and well worth the fall to become mortal. Like him, we must be mystified by the beauty of life.

This story illustrates how much there is to enjoy. I scratch my head and think of all the great adventures us older guys can still muster up. Maybe we go camping, fishing, rent a Winnebago, or fly to Hawaii and climb into the craters of molten rock. Or maybe just hang out around the North Shore at Pipeline. Maybe we can't surf, but it sure is great to watch the thrill of the ones who can while we inhale the salty air and feel the wind across your face. It beats watching television, that's for sure. Get out and buy season tickets for sporting events, concerts, plays, and even the ballet. Live!

Can you experience the pure beauty of life on this planet the way you did as a child? Of course you can, in fact you can do better! You have so much more knowledge and appreciation of how the world turns. Your body is headed toward ultimate freedom, so why not your mind? You can rediscover everything that's available. Go listen to the sound of the ocean and watch the burnt-orangey-red sunrises and sunsets that start and end every day. From how green the grass is to guessing the shapes of clouds, you still have an imagination. Let it soar!

It's inspiring to look at life this way, and when I stop being inspired, it's time to pack it in. Yeah! That's a good quote. I was inspired when I was young, so why not now? In fact, it should be easier. Because I'm old, I know the things I like and what I dislike. I'll go directly to "GO" and collect the $200, then spend it on capturing life.

Okay, but maybe I don't have a lot of disposable income, or I'm not physically able to do everything. So I adapt. I take my portable chair and watch some kids playing soccer or baseball down at the local field. I relish in their achievements and failures, and while I'm doing that, I see ants in the grass, I smell the flowers, pick some dandelions, and feel the breeze. I also watch the younger maniacal parents yelling at the ref or ump, their kids, and each other. I flashback to when I was one of those fanatics (with all my testosterone intact) and seem to remember some old geezers sitting in beat-up lawn chairs laughing at me.

You get the picture. Its ideas from *The Bucket List,* the movie in which Jack Nicholson and Morgan Freeman set out to live life to the fullest in their retirement years. Point being, that age is proportional to what's in your head. You can experience a lot of things in spite of being older, and if you keep love and nature in the forefront of your mind, you'll really enjoy yourself.

***

When I was in my twenties, I told a good friend of mine, "If anyone ever tells me to be more mature or act my age, then he should slap me, 'cause that's the day I begin to die." Living is for the living, and a little love along the way makes the living easier.

Engage in life and all that surrounds you, and you will be set free. Sharing and loving go hand in hand, especially if you experience it with someone who you care for. And now that big T is on the decline and you don't need to get laid or start a war, these final years are your chance at a peaceful swan song. But can both sexes see eye to eye as we age?

Let's examine an older couple who had been together for more than thirty years. They survived raising their kids, and many ups and down. You'd think their years of debating and consenting to points of view would give them a chance to see things as one. Let's take a look.

The woman, who was fifty plus, turned to her husband on one of their ritualistic hand-holding daily walks and asked, "If we weren't married, would you consider me a good friend?" The husband squeezed her hand and immediately answered with a smile. "Of course," he said. "You're my best friend. You bring a calming and insightful point of view into my life. I respect everything about you."

The wife was at a complete loss for words. How could her husband answer so quickly and decisively positive when a lot of her memories revolved around years of arguing and frustration on many levels? She was hard-pressed to believe him, even angry at how his memory seemed so selective.

> IT SEEMS WOMEN GET WRAPPED UP IN EMOTION AND FEEL MORE.

It seems women get wrapped up in emotion and feel more. They experience more happiness, more sadness, more anxiety, and more frustration than us. Let me expand on that. For example, they hold onto their feelings for a longer time and take longer to let them go. Perhaps it's because they don't expel their anger physically, or they're too afraid to lash out and cause pain. So they internalize to avoid confrontation. This is the opposite of a man. Most men have some sort of physical release built into their lives and most love a good confrontation, whether it's an argument or a fight. It's all about testosterone and the competitive nature of men.

Nevertheless, arguments will happen even when people are in love. When a woman verbally attacks her man, his first instinct is verbal retaliation, but if she pushes him to the wall, the confrontation boils up batches of T. This causes a switch to go off in many men. They revert to primal instincts of defend and attack. This reaction results in either a more "in her face" approach or even a physical attack. Not good, either way.

When a man verbally berates a woman, there is little fear

of physical retaliation. So he strikes hard, pounds away, and hurts her. Her only defense is with her mouth. Even though she may strike him, it's no more than a mosquito bite to most men, and they will hit back harder. So the woman can only continue with words, which only escalates the situation. "Hell hath no fury like a woman scorned!" Once this happens, it riles up Mr. T and things get nasty.

The fact is that both of them suffer. When things cool down and T chills out, there's always remorse. I'm certainly not condoning any man hitting a woman, but raging hormones cause imbalance. In women its mood swings; in men it's violence. A lot of men have to go through anger management because of their inability to control the aggressiveness of Mr. T.

The secret is to not let things get out of control and is something all partners need to work at. It's learning how to back off before lightning strikes. Women and men who are determined to get in the last word only add more fuel to the fire. When arguments last too long, it leads to permanent damage in any relationship. So both people must always be thinking about the big picture, the future, and the sunsets together along the sandy beach. There is serenity that comes from meeting in the middle when both parties swallow a bit. The shorter the argument, the less pain and less damage. We need to learn to forgive and forget (just like when we were kids and didn't have all that baggage). And that's the key. It's kind of an unwritten agreement on where the relationship is going, a "oneness" that must be discussed and accepted by both.

> THE SHORTER THE ARGUMENT, THE LESS PAIN AND LESS DAMAGE.

***

In a large percentage of our population, women are dependent on their man, whether they accept it or not. I'm not saying this in a monetary sense. I'm talking about day-in-and-day-out drudgery. Men are good for honey-do lists—the physical and laborious tasks that exist in a home environment. I certainly don't want to stereotype here, but take a look at all the data out there. It's consistent that people are most happy when traditional roles are the norm.

Mentally, women are more in tune with head and heart, but they feel the pain and hold on to it longer. Men, on the other hand are not so cerebral. They feel things instantly and let them go almost as fast. I know what you're thinking: *How can you say that? Men hold grudges forever. They never let go.* That may be true, but usually as it relates to competition. If it's about feelings, men tend to digest and assimilate.

Most long-lasting relationships go through conflict because testosterone breeds competitiveness. Men are simple creatures. When they don't have an agenda, truth flows like a waterfall. Back them into a corner or create an antagonistic environment, and all bets are off when testosterone kicks in.

When men stop competing with their wives, a softer, more relaxed relationship is the by-product. This bodes well for older couples who are still together. It offers days that are happier and in balance. Simply put, there's less to prove and more to enjoy. If we just love each other, then we both win.

We're back to the old adage, "Happy wife! Happy life!" Managing Mr. T can bring contentment. This approach gives true love a chance to succeed.

However, in a lot of marriages the obstacles that cannot be resolved are the very glue that hold them together. It's a sad day when you stop arguing and the relationship crumbles, because you realize conflict has kept you together. When this happens, there is no solution and you need to go your separate ways.

Not everyone is willing to split of course. There are a lot of unhappy older couples out there who will be bitter until the end. Again, their choice. They based their future on dreams and false promises. Because they didn't fess up in time, they are left with an empty world, little love, and no balance anywhere in sight. I hope this is not you, but even if it is, there is good news, still time to change.

> YOU HAVE THE POWER OF FREE WILL.

Change is available every second of every minute, every hour of every day. YOU HAVE THE POWER OF FREE WILL. You have the choice to fall in love again, even if it's with the person who made you angry for all those years. Use that great big eraser to get rid of the hard times and focus on the good times. Start every day with some form of love.

***

I want to talk about passion as we age. Passion is an elusive pursuit. When in a relationship do we lose it?

Three men who worked together were having lunch at a local greasy spoon. The youngest man, Jim, was a newlywed. His face was full of life, and his eyes sparkled. "My wife and I have sex everywhere," he said. "We did it in the zoo, in her car, down at the lake behind this big tree. We've made love in the kitchen, the rec room, even in the upstairs bathroom. We can't stop doing each other."

His coworker, Bruce, who'd been married for seven years, shook his head and laughed. "I remember those days. Now we've got two kids, and we have to book a time to have sex with each other. Then it's in the bedroom with the door closed. We took a vacation last year and made out on the beach, but we were constantly worried someone would see us."

Jim laughed. "Too bad! Don't you miss that raw sexuality?"

"Don't really think about it that way," Bruce shot back. "That's just the way it goes. You'll see."

They both looked over to Paul, the eldest of the three. He deadpanned. "I've been married for forty-four years and have a faint memory of what you two jokers are talking about."

"So," Jim went on. "Do you still have passion for your wife? Do you still have crazy sex?"

"Oh yeah." Paul smirked. "Do we have sex? Only yesterday, we had brief but the most beautiful kind of oral sex."

"Wow!" said Jim. "That's impressive."

"Oh yeah?" Paul said, standing up. "I passed her in the hall-way right outside our bedroom and said, 'SCREW you!'" They all laughed.

"Is it true?" Jim asked. "Is that the kind of passion that's in my future?"

Paul shook his head. "No, I'm kidding, just a joke. But I gotta tell you, there's so much that goes into a long marriage. You go through kids, mortgage payments, bills, struggles, and sickness. Life's a bitch, and it can really crush you."

Jim kept on. "So if that's what marriage turns into, then why stay together?"

"Think about it. When two people are together for such a long time, they know each other like a book. My wife is the only person in the whole wide world that understands and loves me," Paul said. "If it wasn't for her, I wouldn't be the man I am today. I love being around her. Kathy and I don't make love that much anymore, but I've never even considered being with another woman since I fell for her. No woman could make me feel more complete. That's true passion. She's the best lover and best friend I ever had. I'm one lucky man."

> SHE'S THE BEST LOVER AND BEST FRIEND I EVER HAD. I'M ONE LUCKY MAN.

Both Jim and Bruce stared at their older partner, amazed at the soft and gracious words he'd heaped on his wife. They always considered the old guy pretty rough around the edges. After that, they never looked at Paul the same way again. They'd witnessed what older love can aspire to be. It was a future they could attain in the later years of their relationships.

Truth is, there are many reasons to stay in a marriage, but only if it provides both partners with what each other needs. Remember in the chapter "Marriage Material" when Mr. B gave the advice about marrying "the one"? Unfortunately, most marriages are with the 1–8 choices. Hence, most unions go through the motions of initial hot sex, then cooler sex, then kids, then a myriad of situations pulling and pushing on the relationship until there's not a lot of mutually beneficial qualities left.

If mental love does not balance off with physical love, you hit a dead end. There has to be a better reason for continuing the relationship other than kids, the house payments, money—you name it. The only logical reason to stay in a relationship is not money; it's love.

You see, in a long-term relationship that has true love, there's complete honesty, sharing, and mutual respect. Contrary to younger people's ideas of what makes relationships work, such as separate careers, separate vacations, and separate hobbies, the older couples who are truly happy are the ones that used the different phases to grow alongside each other. Then in their "post-kid" years, they appreciate what life offers them together.

There are many documented accounts of older husbands or wives who died of a broken heart months after the first spouse passed on due to loss of purpose and love.

No matter how much testosterone is in your tank, there's no need to hang around this beat-up universe any longer once your true love is gone. You want to get back together as a spark of energy and travel the galaxies as one. It's a great theory, and it makes a certain kind of sense, because in this world we want everything to make sense. That's how we deal with the unknown.

Regardless of the relationship you're in today, first marriage or the fourth, you must do all that's possible to love. You must take the time to love your partner, your children, and your grandchildren no matter what shape your personal direction or health is currently dragging you off in. If you're not in a relationship, then it's even more important to give yourself to the rest of your family and find some love. 'Cause if you want to die happy, then you must have peace and one way to have peace is to care.

Friends become increasingly important as one ages. Mutual relationships have the ability to keep you vibrant, alert, and alive. Simple things like connecting daily by phone, Skype, text, email, and all other forms of communication cement the need to be a functional part of something.

These acts drive and sustain life. We need to feel like there is a future! We need to feel the dream! To attach, create, and do things together is the most basic need alive. I flash to the Tom Hanks movie *Castaway* and see him talking to "Wilson," the inanimate volleyball with a face drawn on it. When "Wilson" floats off to sea, we witness Tom's complete devastation.

We as men, and as humans, need to be in touch. I know that there may be some recluses out there who actually don't want anyone around them. They think they don't want love, but you can only watch so much TV or sleep or live in a cave. You'll be a lot happier if you get with the program and find some friends to hang with. You don't have to fall in love with them, but you can certainly share and show an interest. The alternative is you may just die in your sleep alone and unloved. God save your soul. Maybe you'll have to come back a few times to this low materialistic world to get it right. Let me illustrate the point.

I've was very close to two guys who died for seemingly no particular reason. The first death came early, when I was about twenty. Bobby and I came from a poor neighborhood and goofed around the Community Clubs for kicks. Out of nowhere, he was diagnosed with a brain tumor. He'd been angry lately, moping around the house, and had lost his zip mostly because he'd recently broken up with his childhood sweetheart of four years.

The diagnosis was severe, and the surgeons' decision to operate came quickly. The odds gave him a 1 in 50,000 chance of survival. We were all ecstatic when he made it through. He had only one small complication. His left optic nerve had been touched. This left him cross-eyed, and he had to wear a pirate's patch. He looked cool, but he had no job and no love. He tried to recover by resigning himself to schlepping around the house for two years. He gave up on life. At twenty-two, within the space of three weeks, he got a cold, then bronchitis, and then ultimately died of pneumonia. Go figure. No love, no purpose, and no life.

About ten years ago, it happened again. My friend Chuck,

a guy who owned a huge chicken farm, had a massive heart attack. That's not unusual for someone in their midfifties, but Chuck has this story. We used to tease him about his chickens, 'cause he had a slew of them and serviced the Kentucky Fried Chicken franchise. We called his farm a chicken ranch, and he made millions on those "cluckers." Anyway, right out of high school, he'd had a shotgun wedding and then fathered two more kids with a woman he had "responsibility" to and stuck it out for twenty-two years.

In the aftermath, he got a messy divorce, then went off to pursue the passion and love he thought he'd missed. Chuck had property in Canada, Florida, and California. What better place to find his dream woman?

Young women were all over him. He had lots of dough and was willing to spend a fair chunk to fill in the blanks that had eluded him, but as he wandered in and out of part-time and full-time bicoastal relationships, he never quite found love. He had a lot of hot sex and naked pool parties, but alas, no love. So he checked out with a heart attack at fifty-four. He died while his son was driving him to the airport. No love, no life, no purpose, and no reason to go on.

> NO LOVE, NO LIFE, NO PURPOSE, AND NO REASON TO GO ON.

Of course, it's not always so cut and dried, but it makes you wonder, right?

***

Is there sex after sixty with your current partner? Don't be an idiot. There's a lot of gratifying sex after sixty 'cause Mr. T is still in circulation. Your performance may not be what is has been in the past, but it's more beautiful in other ways.

If you're an older single and you find a new love, I can promise there will still be heart pounding excitement when she walks into the room. Your testosterone levels may even increase slightly. Your pulse will still quicken when you're counting the rings waiting for her to pick up the phone. You'll be dying to catch a glimpse of your new love coming out to meet you. Dating will still be filled with expectation just like way back when. You see, love guarantees the butterflies will flutter in your stomach. It guarantees the ache in your heart when you're apart. It guarantees the anticipation of being together. Love is love, no matter the age.

Once again this reinforces what life is truly about. Love gives balance. Love gives one the gift of living life. Love conquers all, and all you need is love. A wise man said that if you have love in your life, you have more than enough. Getting older creates a need for patience and care, tolerance and cooperation, but most of all it requires understanding and the ability to love and be loved.

So as men age, we give in. Twenty or thirty years ago, we wouldn't be having this conversation. We wouldn't have the knowledge or the tolerance to understand all this talk about love. We might have even been accused of being wimps for being so "lovesick." But that's why we're on the evolution train.

We can confirm that we are born with nothing and we die with nothing. Whatever occurs in between are the experiences we breathe and bleed for. If we reflect on earlier years, we can see where we triumphed and failed, where we loved and hated, where we chose to be combative and where we've given in. If we think back to the moments of love versus disappointments and regrets, I can attest to the fact that we'd

> **CLOSE YOUR EYES AND THINK OF THE MOMENTS YOU FOUND LOVE RIGHT NOW.**

prefer to keep the beautiful loving memories and the conflicts we won with us until the end.

Close your eyes and think of the moments you found love right now. Feel the kindness permeating your body? Compare that to the anxiety you still feel for memories of anger. If you had to choose what we want most as we near death, it's the warmth you're feeling right now.

You might think that all this talk about love has gone to my head and has made me soft. You may think that love is not a manly thing to talk about, but think again. Isn't this exactly where our society wants us to end up? Isn't our society pointing us in the direction of love and compassion? Think about it. If you're honest, then even the most male parts of you will have to agree, and it's a much better place than where we've been.

Scoreboard: Later relationships

Testosterone: Has maxed out and is down trending. Still there for the fight-or-flight response, but even those are diminishing.

Balance: We've made it this far and are now willing to concede that life is pretty simple. Once we've got the primary needs of food and shelter taken care of, we can concentrate on being with the ones we love. We begin to nurture and cherish those relationships for exactly what they are. If we practice what we preach, then we are pretty content and have discovered the key to balance.

Score for this chapter: Half a point more for balance!

Total: Out of balance: 4   In balance: 5

**Finally, with Mr. T withdrawing, have we been able to get a grip on our internal struggle and achieve some balance? It only took the man sixty years or so to start winning this battle. Ladies, show some compassion, will you? At least give us a little credit.

CHAPTER 16

AFTERGLOW

Old age has arrived. You know, seventy, eighty plus, where I can't really touch my toes unless I bring my gnarled-up foot to my hand. I put my socks on sideways with one leg crossed over the other 'cause that's the only way I can. Everything creaks when I move. When I finally get up and dressed, I walk with a little list to the left from an old back injury. It's past the point where my chiropractor can fix it. I've lost a few of inches in height, some hair, and a couple of teeth. They were lower left molars, so I chew on the right. No big deal.

I only sleep four to five hours a night, and I can nap at the drop of a hat. Worst part is, I see my old man every time I look in the mirror, and I admit it scares me a little. Then, I can just laugh. I'm not the only one who sees it that way either.

My wife, kids, and grandkids are all calling me a grumpy grandpa. I go with the flow. Vanity left when humility entered and T ebbed. I'm satisfied with my life. I can hardly keep up, but I buy the little ones butterscotch-dipped ice cream cones, feed them my special dish of french fries and gravy, introduce them to "root beer floats" and let them eat all that unhealthy stuff. I love spoiling the grandkids. It really pisses their parents off, but it's all good.

I'm thinking back over the years and all the predicaments. It's ridiculous how I strived for material gains and chased women, jobs, and titles. All the previous chapters with their massive amounts of Mr. T, where is it all now? Ha!

By the way, if you look down and can't see your feet, then you gotta laugh. That bulge you first noticed when you saw your profile in the mirror during your late forties has made a permanent home underneath your ribcage. It's expanded quite nicely over time. It's been a big financial investment to achieve it, and we're way past trying to suck it in.

Maybe a Chuck Norris and Cindy Crawford workout will get the T pumping through your veins one final time, but don't get a heart attack trying, okay? It's a joke. Relax. Go for slow walks. Keep the blood moving.

As men get over their physical demise, they only have events and friendships for comfort, and that shouldn't surprise anyone. For no matter where you end up, you are with the crowd or the wife you're supposed to be with. Make no mistake, you should be really happy about your current place.

You see, when you reach old age, if you're broke and broken, miserable and angry at the world, you should stop and reflect. You've had decades

> I GUARANTEE THAT IF YOU HONESTLY LOOK BACK IN THE 20/20 REARVIEW MIRROR, YOU WILL BE ABLE TO CLEARLY IDENTIFY PRETTY MUCH EVERY MAJOR CHOICE YOU CONSCIOUSLY MADE.

where you made specific choices to get to this point. Whether you believe in destiny or not, it is inconsequential. I guarantee that if you honestly look back in the 20/20 rearview mirror, you will be able to clearly identify pretty much every major choice you consciously made. Those are the choices that put you on the beat-up, pissed-off road that you walk today. Well done, you have only yourself to blame.

Whether it's about taking or quitting a job at the right or wrong time, having kids when you weren't quite ready, getting into that car accident, getting caught stealing at the drug store, being too drunk too many times, and on and on and on. Every single example above was a conscious choice you made and has catapulted you on to your own personal crapper.

On the other hand, if you're wealthy, still married to the sexiest woman alive, have a gaggle of great-grandchildren, and can hang out at the yacht club where you play tennis and golf at a whim, then you deserve that too.

Either way, you have to rejoice. Mission accomplished. You are a success at what you set out to be. Congrats and kudos.

Oh. You'd rather be the rich guy with the yacht? You mean you're not that happy with where you are in spite of your choices? Perhaps you had some bad luck or mitigating circumstances that took you down the dark and lonely road. Is that your excuse? Please, spare me. Shape up and be a man. Everyone experiences both good and bad luck in their seventy or eighty plus years of living.

There are tons of guys who went to jail, did drugs, had crappy jobs, grew up in the ghetto, or were too small, stupid, or fat who came out on the other side and made something of themselves. You don't have to go far or think too hard to rattle off their names, do you? So no matter what's on your current plate, make peace with your mess and make choices today that will stay with you until the end. Get happy, you old relic. Stop your finger pointing.

***

When I was in my early twenties, while everyone was driving Fords and Chevys, I made a choice and spent every dollar I could get my hands on to buy a Triumph Spitfire from one of my phys-ed university professors. It was a really cool green British import.

This baby sports car was quite rare where I grew up and, in fact, was the first one I'd ever seen. It was the same for many. When I drove with the top down through the streets, almost everyone smiled as I went by. It was a cool curiosity. It gave me great joy, made me feel special, and got me noticed.

One of the first trips I drove it on was to Chicago. I went for a dual track meet where I was representing my university and running the men's hurdles. Another event that weekend was a synchronized swim meet going on at the pool.

After a long day of competition, I approached the parking lot between the two facilities. There, checking out my ride were five beautifully tanned babes in South Florida sweat suits. Of course, this gave me the opportunity to start chatting. They wanted me to give them a ride back to their hotel, but alas, it was a two-seater. I did a quick up and down, and after some mild flirting picked Wendy, a dark-haired, dark-eyed, broad-shouldered beauty.

The two of us ended up spending a lot of time together and even better than that, her team adopted me as their mascot for the rest of the meet. We dined and bar-hopped together for three nights, and the girls all treated me like royalty. I was among fifteen brazen babes and pretty much could've had anyone I wanted, but I was a gentleman and controlled Mr. T. As it turned out, I really got to like Wendy and promised that I'd drive down to be with her in St. Petersburg, Florida, once school was over.

Wendy attended SFU at Tampa. While there, I went to a few of their practices at a local pool. I was infatuated with her great body and even more impressed as I watched her swim underwater for four laps.

We spent a couple of weeks together, then I drove back penniless, my credit cards maxed out. Was I looking forward to doing it again? You bet your ass. We wrote, phoned, and sent audio tapes back and forth for the next six months while I tried to recover financially. When I decided to go see her again, I had big plans.

My green Spitfire had now been upgraded to a brand-new maroon Triumph TR6 with electric overdrive. Step back. Watch out! "Six and the Single Man" was the ad slogan up on the 20x10 billboard at the dealers. I was all of that.

I figured if a puny little Spitfire could get me the likes of Wendy, then what would TR6 bring forth? I filled up with gas and hit the road for the two-and-a-half day drive from Winnipeg, Manitoba, Canada to St. Petersburg, Florida, USA.

When I got there, she was blown away and loved the new car. She got me to drive her all over town while she showed me and the car off to everyone she could find. As the days passed, we spent most of our time at the pool where she was a life-guard, then passed the breezy warm nights walking the Gulf Coast and skinny dipping. We went camping, restaurant hopping, and made out a lot; however, she wouldn't let me have sex with her. I knew something was wrong.

On the second to last day of my visit, the shit hit the fan. She confessed to an old case of boyfriend blues. Seems her grade-school sweetheart, and Mommy's favorite potential son-in-law, had been drafted, and his Air Force time in New Mexico was up next month. To my chagrin, he was coming home. Wendy expressed quietly to me that she owed it to herself and her mom to give him another shot.

My head began to spin, and I could feel the anger inching up my spine.

New car, my ass, I thought. *What did all that glitter and debt do for me lately?* Her pretty little face was full of tears with "I love you, but …."

"Yeah, yeah, yeah."

I got a big kiss goodbye from the teary-eyed Wendy. I packed up. I was a total mess. I left her parents' cobblestone driveway lined with ripened tomato plants in a hurry to get back home.

What a chump! I said to myself while her mom waved me good riddance with a smile as wide as the Gulf of Mexico.

I drove back to the 'Peg in my shiny red convertible and sulked through a dozen states, six interstates, and three tollways until I declared myself a Canadian citizen at the border. Once I was across the border, I put the pedal to the metal, and opened up the dual Stromberg carburetors. When I hit the last portion of undivided highway, I finally eased up as the city came into view. All I could think about was how green the grass was all the way to my mother's home.

As I turned onto her street and pulled up to the curb, the anger was still with me. I got out and slammed the car door. My neighbor Dan, a guy I grew up and went to school with, came out in the street to greet me.

"Wow! Great car," he said. "I really envy you. Your mom said you'd been down in Florida with some hot babe."

"Too hot!" I replied as I jumped out onto the fender. "She had issues."

He stood by the car, his reflection beaming off the side panel while he admired the interior and stroked the leather. "You're so lucky," he went on. "You get to drive all over the place anytime you want, and you have this amazing car. You really know how to live. I wish I could do what you do, but I'm totally stuck in a rut."

I was scratching my head. "You can do it too," I reassured him.

"No, I can't," he said. "I have a full-time job, got to work, got to save, and can't get away."

"Sure, you can," I implored. "Anyone can. You only have to decide to do it, and away you go, it's done. It might cost you a little, but you have your whole life to make money, right?"

"That's pretty risky," he said. "I could never do it. I need to save."

"Save?" I shot back. "You mean like money in the bank?"

"Yeah. Few thousand. I'm looking at buying some property for me and Debbie. We're thinking about getting married." His eyes lit up again. "Gosh, I really envy you. You don't have anything holding you back. You're free."

"Free, you say?" I giggled. "You want my debt? My pain? I just came back from a three-thousand-mile waste of time where I got dumped for a draftee. I got no savings. My car was bought on a loan. My gas and credit cards are totally maxed out." I held out my car keys. "You want to trade? My freedom for your rut?"

He never even reached for the keys. "No thanks." He smiled while wagging his head from side to side. "I need to be financially safe for Debbie and me."

I watched him head across the street to his mom's house. "Sure you don't want to switch? Last chance," I called out.

"I'm sure." He stopped at the sidewalk and turned. "But I

really do envy you." He saluted, then smiled. "You got balls."

I stuffed the keys in my pocket.

So what does that story have to do with the "afterglow"? Perception and reality are never what they seem to be, and as we age toward imminent death, we need to get it.

- Need to see things for what they are.

- Need to admit our strengths and weaknesses.

- Need to be what a man is supposed to be: namely, a strong role model our kids can look up to and be proud of no matter what our lot in life has thrown us.

- Need to have dignity.

We also need our "later in life" testosterone to help us balance the world while we wait for the inevitable. We need to focus on what is true and important, despite all the creaking bones, disease, and disappointments. Finally, we must stand up and accept what we have accomplished. And that is what a man is, pure and simple. Perhaps Popeye says it best, "I am what I am. That's all that I am." This doesn't mean we should be rebellious or confrontational. It doesn't mean we have to change necessarily, but it does mean that we have to represent what we hold dearest in our hearts and minds.

Men all have a dream when they are young. It is branded into their genes from the get-go. It's about winning with honor, courage, strength, morality, and of course sex. These attributes make real men, tried and true! This is what we should measure ourselves (minus the sex) for in the afterglow.

Methinks that this old timer, with his wisdom and experience, is almost exactly what our North American male is supposed to be as a younger man on the hunt. He has the best of the male traits. No violence, no corruption, but still strong

> ISN'T THIS WHAT EVERY WOMAN DREAMS THAT HER MAN WILL BE LIKE?

and assertive. No overt testosterone, yet he has compassion, tolerance, and care.

Isn't this the male persona we are looking for? Isn't this what every woman dreams that her man will be like? I think the answer in many ways is yes. As man ages, his need for control, power, and wealth should give way to peace, not anger. Isn't that where you'd like to be near the end? Don't you yearn for peace, freedom, and love with those around you?

Take a deep breath and let it out slowly. When you relax with these thoughts, you can only go in one direction, one of serenity. At any age, this space can put you in a really beautiful state of mind. (Maybe I'll try meditation; it's just a thought, a fleeting one, but nevertheless a possibility.) Peace and love. It was the cry of the "flower children" of the sixties. Maybe it's not such a bad idea! We just have to keep it real. Take away the drugs and noncommitment that those hippies had, and it's a pretty fantastic way to go.

It certainly gives old T a chance to relax and enjoy his later days.

Scoreboard: Afterglow

Testosterone: Testosterone level at this point is low. And who cares anyway—you're not in a position to fight or hunt for sex.

Balance: With the right frame of mind we've made it. We are at one with the universe.

Score for this chapter: Balance supreme!

Total: Out of balance: 4   In balance: 6

CHAPTER 17

TESTOSTERONE'S LAST GASP

What's left to talk about? Is there testosterone in man's future? Of course there is. It has been and always will be the distinguishing hormone for all men. Until natural selection blends the sexes to something resembling some kind of bisexual hermaphrodite, men will have a lot more of Mr. T than women. And God bless men for that, because without Mr. T, we would be a wet mass of sniveling protoplasm unable to stand up to manual labor, aggression, or danger.

Let's stay true to the real issue here: the one of balance. Right from childhood, men are waging a constant battle—an inner war of self-control that if left unchecked could explode at any time. Due to society's protocol and the "taken for granted status" and the "you have to be tough to be a man" idiom, our hero is changing to a more tranquil state. The end result of that alteration will be directly proportional to the expectations North American culture continues to heap on our hero over time. Nevertheless, our homeboy has mellowed significantly into the twenty-first century, and I will show you proof below.

***

In general, guys don't bitch or moan about the rules of equality in mixed company. We know better. We do it among ourselves on golf courses, in locker rooms and gyms. The instant we do it in public, we are tagged as pigs, chauvinistic, insensitive, non-caring, and out of touch human beings.

> HOWEVER, MEN HAVE BOWED AND ACCEPTED THAT TODAY'S EMANCIPATED WOMEN ARE ABLE TO SAY AND DO PRETTY MUCH ANYTHING THEY LIKE.

However, men have bowed and accepted that today's emancipated women are able to say and do pretty much anything they like. Hence, as obliging partners, we have to take it whether we like it or not. That's progress one more time (as if you haven't gotten it by now).

Currently, women have hit full stride and have the upper hand in sex and pretty much all social aspects of our day-in-and-day-out functions. Men are not upset at watching women take the reins and be outspoken—not at all. We are happy for women's gains and are being extremely patient while they find their niche. We also accept this behavior because we want and desire a better, less violent world. By definition, we know this can happen if and only if we participate and value women as true partners.

Cut to the loud obnoxious woman who dominates social gatherings. She is becoming more seen than heard and has a strong opinion which she's not afraid to blurt out. Men look at these women with a touch of "been there, done that, it ain't a big deal" syndrome.

There were lots of loud, obnoxious cigar-smoking men once upon a time, so why shouldn't some women take on the role too? Equality is at work. Men are used to handling that. We either shout back sarcastic jabs or walk away. Among men, this type of rhetoric is commonplace, and it glides past us like a hot knife through butter.

Many women display behaviors that would get a man's ass kicked. However, this kind of woman doesn't intimidate us. And this is a key point. Men don't want to compete with women on a man's level. We are waiting for the flak to disperse on all the revolutionary fronts. We're waiting, and hoping, that society will once again need and love men for who they are.

> MAN LONGS FOR THE OPPORTUNITY TO BE MALE, TO BE A LITTLE MACHO WITH A TOUCH OF SENSITIVITY AND CHIVALRY.

Man longs for the opportunity to be male, to be a little macho with a touch of sensitivity and chivalry. What he is discovering is that a lot of women want the same. We have evolved.

You see, most of our traditional male opinions have already been squashed by society's new rules. Man is relegated to expressing himself in areas like the aforementioned golf course or the clubhouse (something like a designated "man" area).

If our hero wants to succeed in the new millennium with

Mr. T intact, he must once again rise to the occasion, because in the end, competition and prolongation of the species is what it's all about. There is no denying that man wants to be successful on this new battlefield. Therefore, he must keep his animal instincts in check, yet he must be brilliant if he wants to keep his place in the social order. This competitive edge, inherent in all males, guarantees Mr. T will endure under increasingly stringent parameters.

***

Let's talk about real and well-documented opposites. A large percentage of women would be happy to say that men are cold and unattached. They accuse men for their lack of compassion and care, but just think about it for a moment. Men have been thrust into battle since their cavemen days. Decade after decade, they have been the ones soaked in blood, experiencing the brutality of combat and death.

While the majority of women took care of the children and mourned their losses, it has been the male who had to endure the severing of limbs, gutted corpses, bullet-riddled bodies, and the stench of rotting flesh. Many men witnessed their best friends and comrades disintegrating in front of their eyes. Only recently has the horrifying scenes of combat been shared with the fairer sex.

Over the centuries, this singular fact hardened man genetically through the natural selection process. He was conditioned to go, despite the horrors and debauchery of war, to defeat the enemy. "Real men don't cry" is one of the most used clichés in our language. So I think we can forgive the current versions of our hero to a large extent for not being as compassionate as women.

IT MAKES PERFECT SENSE THAT MEN CRY LESS AND MOVE ON FASTER THAN WOMEN.

While men were ripping each other's hearts out and decapitating one another on the battlefield, their women were back at the ranch consoling each other for the husbands who didn't come back. It makes perfect sense that men cry less and move on faster than women. It's a matter of survival. No time for compassion or fair play in war. Not if you want to stay alive.

If and when battle-hardened women experience hand-to-hand mortal combat, I'm wondering if they'll show the same kind of resolve. I'm wondering if they would be showing compassion and fair play while aiming their rifle at the man (or woman) who just took out six of their best friends.

There is no doubt that we should admire our veterans for living with the horrors of what they've witnessed defending our freedoms. In the last half-century, in spite of war after war, the majority of our men have taken a step back from this approach. Despite their natural instincts, they are learning to control T and have been able to find a softer balance in a relatively short span of time.

We are extremely fortunate that modern warfare has never been fought on North American soil. The United States and Canadian governments have worked relentlessly to keep it that way. Our women have never had to see firsthand the perils of war. I hate to say this, but North American women still have no idea about that kind of world. It's easy for them to want everything to be fair and equal when they don't have to physically defend it. Past generations of our veterans have made sure of those liberties with their lives.

There is good and evil in the world and our men stand up

to evil. The blatant attacks of the twin towers on 9/11 are only one example of this. It is a modern-day miracle that since those landmarks went down at ground zero, the terrorist movement has not been able to mount another blow between the Atlantic and Pacific Oceans. Why has this not happened? Well, it took some courage and balls to go after the instigators of the attack. It took action to go over there.

For all of his perceived shortcomings, George W. Bush's days at the White House will reflect one thing in the history books. Since 9/11, George had the testosterone to go to the source. He was able to keep that war over there for the remainder of his presidency. Right or wrong, moral or not, that is an indisputable fact. This same philosophy was followed up by President Obama and because of their strength, our land has been spared the daily suicide bombings, torture, raping, kidnapping, and death that we see every day on every news network. That's pretty impressive seeing that we all know the bad guys are among us, lurking in major cities across the nation. I'm sure they are preparing, waiting for us to get weak and lazy.

Unmitigated and radical aggression is one area that men completely understand. They've been dealing with it since time began. They know the world isn't fair, and they know they must make sacrifices to defend and keep our freedoms alive and well.

No matter what system you believe in, whether its capitalism, communism, or socialism, the struggle is all about basic needs and power. As long as there is disparity in the world, there will be self-righteous agendas, extremism, and political BS with world leaders.

Whoever is on the right side of victory determines who gets the spoils. It is men who start and end wars. Can you remember a conflict where women did all the fighting? Of course not! Even with modern weaponry, there would be a problem, because sooner or later, you got to get it done on the ground, hand to hand.

It's all good to think we can change the world to be a better place by example, but our freedoms and mutual respect do not meet the criteria of other leaders and other societies. The best we can hope for is some kind of harmony. Testosterone will be in the mix, one way or another.

One last thing. Because of the lack of international conflict and high-level of human rights on our soil, there are so many bleeding hearts in our system. Since Pearl Harbor, generations who live peacefully in their homes have never had to fight a real life or death enemy. This is because our leaders (predominantly men) had the strength, courage, and self-confidence, all aided by testosterone, to keep our enemies away.

Current female politicians, school teachers, and stay-at-home moms have never had to see their friends, neighbors, and homes being bombed. They've never been subjected first-hand to random killing, torture, and maiming of loved ones. They've never had to make the tough calls. Only recently have our women been able to choose to defend our country against foreign and domestic enemies (another merit for equality).

However, the ones who don't volunteer or choose to serve cry over the books that have surfaced about women in other countries who have no liberties, who are abused, tortured, and killed just for being a woman. They empathize, want to help, stand up for their abused sister's rights but have no idea how it is in those lands. The men in those lands are ruthless and control their women by fear and death. It is so easy to talk about how they suffer. Talk is cheap in our society, in a system which has such a liberal constitution. I'm not saying we shouldn't be standing side by side trying to make those changes, but the real push must come from within each and every society. Change can only start when men work together with women to make it happen.

What do we really know about the atrocities of other countries when the closest we'll ever come is perhaps a drive-by shooting? When you're on the outside looking in, the glass is pretty foggy. From Darfur to Tehran, from Baghdad to the West Bank, we witness the terror unfold on CNN. However, that is only a fleeting glimpse into their pain. We watch for a couple of moments, cut to commercial, change the channel, or turn it off. We have the choice. They live it 24/7. To exist in their world, testosterone is compulsory, as is strength and the ability to endure and overcome.

The concept of suggesting that a hormone secreted from the brain may drive political leaders to wage battles and help war-stricken individuals overcome hardship is perhaps pushing the envelope, but take Mr. T away and what do you have left? I may be giving testosterone too much credit, but as a man I wouldn't want to be without it.

It's just a matter of time before fanatical religions and radical maniacs start the final battle. When the suicide bombing and martyrdom happens, and push comes to shove, men will be the ones who will dig in. Men are combat driven by instinct, and armed conflict has no rules.

Testosterone is the hormone of choice for confrontation, and I think we all agree that being a little out of balance would only help our survival. Should we send an army of women with the best equipment possible to wage war? An interesting thought to consider. Let's ask around and see what the general population thinks about that idea. Or should we turn the other cheek?

From the North American point of view, our military men, and now our women, want to defend our freedom on whatever continent our enemies choose to challenge us. Like a dog hunting its kill, we will succeed. Mr. T will lead the way. And that's a good thing for our guys.

He's always led the way. From George Washington and our fight with the British, all the way through two World Wars, Korea, Vietnam, and now the War on Terror. If our men hadn't embraced the power of T, standing up to any and all invaders, I shudder to think of where our free and beautiful land would be right now.

> MEN NEED TESTOSTERONE TO FIGHT MEN BECAUSE MEN POSE THE GREATEST DANGER.

Men need testosterone to fight men because men pose the greatest danger. For the last few decades, men could only get their fix of hand-to-hand violence from professional football and boxing. Joe Lewis, Sugar Ray, Mike Tyson, Joe Frazier, George Foreman, and Muhammad Ali were at the epicenter of maleness and believe me, they were the rage. Don King promoted his way to millions while he featured these household icons of maleness. Presently, that's why the UFC and the MMA events are gaining so much popularity, especially among men. Most women find both sports too violent, and question why they should be allowed on television. Aren't Wrestlemania and the NFL enough?

Well, to be sure, the NFL is a fixture on most men's Sunday calendar come fall. That speaks for itself. But let's face it, for real men, WWE's best part is the women pummeling each other in a good cat fight or in the mud. We like seeing pretty women body slamming each other in bikinis. Granted, the men are strong and athletic, but the brutality part is lame. It's just entertainment.

But on the serious side, real men have been gravitating to the UFC experience. They need to feel that kind of release because they intrinsically feel the pain; they can identify being in the Octagon. They need to know that nothing in there is fake. True, there may be some casualties, but then again, that's life. If you want to fight, then you accept the risk. It's truly a man's sport. The bare knuckles and kicks to the head are fantastic. They are at war.

***

In 1975, James Caan played Jonathon E., a futuristic hero in the film *Rollerball*. It was a combination of roller derby meets football meets Running Man. The game revolves around scoring goals while trying to beat down their opponent. As the season hit the playoffs, the rules gradually disappeared. The finals pit two teams against one another. The object: to score more goals and totally eliminate the opposition.

There were no guns, only the combatants on a track with roller skates and motorcycles. The crowds went wild with every score and every player eliminated. Until Jonathon E. was all alone. His brain, athletic ability, and Mr. T had given him the victory. The crowd chanted "Jonathon! Jonathon!" as he circled the track for the winning goal. He was the last man standing. Perhaps the future doesn't stray all that far from the gladiator days of past.

Outside of the ring or arena, and back in our homes and businesses, we must be thankful for Mr. T.

God bless testosterone so our men can be strong, assertive, protective, and male.

> GOD BLESS THE FACT THAT WITHIN OUR BORDERS, OUR MEN HAVE LEARNED BALANCE AND THE ABILITY TO MANAGE TESTOSTERONE.

God bless the men who are willing to defend our women, country, and the strong values of integrity, honor, and pride that free men in a civilized world stand for.

God bless the fact that within our borders, our men have learned balance and the ability to manage testosterone. They've allowed a vast majority of their women to stand beside them without putting them down, sexually or physically.

Here's a statistic that proves Mr. T is in balance and under control: The Bureau of Justice Statistics states, "Domestic violence in the United States declined significantly from 1993 to 2004, with nonfatal incidents dropping more than 50 percent." There you have it.

God bless our men for the fortitude, acceptance, and forward thinking to allow our women equality on pretty much all levels. Our men willingly do this so we can conquer the immense challenges of future adversities with a single and powerful mind.

God bless the men who can see the future in a balanced world of love and equal rights. And God bless our men who use their testosterone to focus on making the world a better and more loving place for all.

God bless our men, for without these kinds of values, we would all still be living back in the Middle Ages!

Scoreboard: Testosterone's last gasp

Testosterone: Testosterone levels have come and gone. We see and acknowledge the need to possess this hormone to keep the world in a state of balance. As long as men are losing control of Mr. T, only soldiers with Mr. T. can get them under control.

Balance: The struggle never ends, but we in North American are leading the way across the globe and setting a new standard for the management of male aggression.

Score for this chapter: It's not a scoring chapter, yet we are witnessing a better version of our hero!

Total: Out of balance: 4   In balance: 6

CHAPTER 18

DO WOMEN NEED MEN AT ALL?

A woman was sitting in the bar of an expensive hotel enjoying an after-work cocktail when a tall, exceptionally handsome, sexy middle-aged man sat down two stools away. He was so striking that the woman found herself staring at him.

The man couldn't help but notice her overtly attentive ogle. He smiled and stared back, as any man would. Realizing how vulnerable this made her caused a crimson blush to appear on her cheeks. She was about to apologize, but before she got a word out, he walked over and whispered in her ear, "I'll do anything, absolutely anything you want me to do, no matter how kinky, for twenty dollars."

Flabbergasted, the woman pulled back but was met with his calming blue eyes. She could feel her heart pounding, genuinely intrigued by his offer. He leaned in once more, close enough for her to smell his musky cologne. "Anything for a mere twenty dollars, but there's one condition."

Her senses heightened, the woman brushed his cheek with hers and whispered in his ear, "What is this one condition?"

The man pulled back, but only far enough so their noses were able to inhale each other's sweetness. He became more assertive. "You have to tell me what to do in just three words."

The woman closed her eyes.

He could see a slight tremble in her lips and could only imagine what rapturous thoughts were playing out inside her head. He noticed her hand inching ever so slowly to the opening of her purse.

She took one more look into those ocean-blue eyes, then pulled a crisp twenty from her wallet, along with a pen and a small piece of paper. She now had his complete attention. "I'm going to write down my address," she said.

"No need." He shook his head. "I'll be happy to pay for the best suite in this hotel."

She considered his proposition, smiled, and went back to writing. "I don't want to cheapen the experience."

He smiled, nodding in an understanding way and could feel the excitement.

She reached for his palm and pressed the bill and the small yellow paper into it, then folded his fingers over the note one by one.

He looked down at his fist, barely able to conceal his anticipation. "Okay, I've got the money and the address, but you forgot the condition."

The woman got up and pulled out a set of Lexus car keys. "No, I didn't, and do you mind if I drive?"

The man shrugged. "Not at all, but I'm still waiting for those three little words."

Hardly able contain to her excitement, she put her hand right in front of his face and made the come closer sign with her forefinger. As he moved in, she put her hand on the back of his neck and pulled him to her, pressing her breasts against his chest and placing her lips right on his ear. She could feel their thighs touching through the satin lining on her dress.

"I'm waiting." He nearly choked on his words.

She squeezed the nape of his neck gently, then ran her fingertips through his hair.

He arched toward her, his hips pressing softly into hers.

She closed her eyes and whispered, "Clean my house."

Okay, maybe you saw that one coming, maybe not. The story may be lame, but it serves to illustrate an important point: men and women are remarkably different. Regardless, men have surrendered. Women have made it to the big leagues. They've conquered the school system, boardroom, and bedroom, and they're even flying fighter jets and going into space. They've boldly gone where no women have gone before, and it seems the sky is the limit. Despite of all this, men have given them the thumbs-up and encouraged them to be all they can be. As a result of these progressions, I believe that it's possible that our society may be on its way to a potentially true matriarchal society.

This kind of social order may exalt women to the pinnacle of power and respect they've only dreamed about. It may spawn a world where the male species will be relegated to physical labor, entertainment in the form of sports and music, and procreation. Who knows, perhaps women may begin to discard inferior male babies, so that female offspring can emulate Wonder Woman or Laura Croft.

But what the hey? Women are getting to the top of their game. Pro-activists are quick to point out all the virtues that women bring to the table. They can show us document after document about how women in the workplace typically run most if not all businesses, and how businesses thrive because of the work ethic of women. They can also show us acknowledged proof that banks are more willing to loan money to women because they actually pay that money back.

Perhaps all of the above is because of the innate nurturing that comes along with motherhood. Once they give birth, there is no choice. With or without the father, she must feed, care for, and bring up their offspring. This forces women to be more responsible, more reliable, more compassionate, more giving. Men, on the other hand, often walk away from their responsibilities in business and child-rearing. So what's left? Is a world without men in vital positions possible?

Take away their role in procreation and manual labor and maybe the answer is a resounding yes. Let's take a look at what our society is faced with today. Childbearing years for women tend to be thirty-five and under. Is having a man for sex a necessary part of an aging women's needs? I can see a lot of women liking this question, because the answer is probably no. On the other hand, we all know what men will answer. Another example of our differences.

***

Have you heard of the "Marital Muscle"? Here's the deal. You're going out with a girl. The sex and the time together are unprecedented. You fall hopelessly in love. You search the diamond stores, find the perfect ring, propose, and place an engagement ring on her finger. This is where the

> HAVE YOU HEARD OF THE "MARITAL MUSCLE"?

"Marital Muscle" begins. From that moment, she will have sex with you anywhere, anytime, and anyhow. The man is in a state of bliss.

Then, your wedding day arrives. You place a second ring on the same finger. This begins to deactivate the Marital Muscle. Slowly but surely, over a six-month to two-year period, sex becomes less and less frequent. After that, the only thing that can reactivate the "Marital Muscle" is guilt, the pursuit of having a child, a lavish vacation, or a serious shopping spree. Is this a fair assessment? Sexist, yes. Overgeneralized? Guilty as charged, but likely more true than not.

It seems that once women have "done their duty" to procreate and get the marriage commitment, what's left? Well, about fifty to sixty years without a practical need for sex. So physically, is there a sexual sanctuary for men after they've said "I do" or help make babies? Or does man's continued fixation on getting laid just get in the way? Do women crave or need sex once they've gotten older? I'm not a woman, but I assume they need some kind of physical satisfaction. If that's the case, then the only debate is how much is enough, and do they require a man at all?

> BEHIND MOST GREAT MEN, THERE'S A GREAT WOMAN, AND BEHIND MOST GREAT WOMEN, THERE'S A GREAT MAN.

If it's purely a pursuit of pleasure, they can turn off the lights, get out the toys, and handle that on their own. What is so preferable or compelling about having your own personal man that many women still desire? As we both age, it ain't about the sex. Is it perhaps about cuddling, holding hands, sharing, being each other's best friend?

Here is something you can bet the ranch on. Behind most

great men, there's a great woman, and behind most great women, there's a great man. To reach the status of greatness, the person must stand the test of time. This is well documented through history. So there must be a logical reason why we are better together than alone.

Let's start with the brain. I googled a few facts about brains and mental differences, and here's what I came up with. Men have nearly 6.5 times the amount of gray matter related to general intelligence than a woman, whereas women have nearly 10 times the amount of white matter related to intelligence compared to men. Most men have "spatial ability." That is why they can rotate a map in their mind and navigate afterward from memory. This is because (anthropologically speaking) men needed to find their way home with the food to ensure the survival of the family. Women stayed in the cave with the kiddies and didn't have to worry about directions. Men weren't cerebral unless they were trying to capture prey for food or for sex.

Early men also desired a singular mate to ensure his child would be genetically his. The best way of doing this was to leave her in a place and guard her so she didn't get the chance to stray. Man's natural instinct is to fight first, ask questions later. They also would prefer to have sex with a different woman every day, but to safeguard his relationship (and secure his progeny) he has been forced into a pattern of monogamy. At least in our society it starts out that way.

Most women don't get along with directions. In fact, most women don't know if they came in from the left or right side of a department store or mall. In hotels, there's a 50/50 chance that they'll turn the wrong way when exiting an elevator. On the other hand, what women bring to the table tends to be the driving force behind civilizations and other domesticated items. They offer reason without chopping each other's head off. The more educated women become, the more they impact a kinder and more enriched society.

So it seems each has landed a specific role with a definitively positive impact. Thus, when we put them together in a social situation, good things can happen because they depend on each other for the betterment of the union. When men are left unchecked with their barbaric and rude traits, can women really put up with us? Do they always want to be the calming force behind us? Perhaps women could live in the absence of an opposite sex partner.

Let's see what the eggheads say. Sociologists at Virginia University found the majority of both sexes are happiest in traditional marriages. Those are the ones that run on old-fashioned gender lines, where the man is the main bread-winner. Regardless of what married women say, they tend to have happier marriages when their husband is a good provider. Happiest of all were women whose husbands brought in at least two-thirds of the household income. Helping with domestic chores was more or less irrelevant. In short, it seems women currently do not feel truly comfortable earning more than their men. The need to rely on a man is driven by such a deep-seated biological urge that most theorists cannot see it ever being completely eradicated.

So let's get this straight. First of all, men are completely in the dark about the negative feelings that women conceal due to earning power. I mean, isn't equality what women fought, bled, and died for? Now that they've got it, they realize it's not the panacea they'd hoped for. Secondly, where do we draw the line?

Let's go back in time to when the man made the money and paid for the lifestyle, including all the extras. He had no problem giving his woman whatever she craved as long as it didn't kill the budget. In fact, he was happy to do it. It was his side of the bargain. He never complained about it. It was the man's job.

Then progress happened. Money became an issue as TV marketing splashed out lavish bobbles. It affected the marriage by demanding more. Many men couldn't afford the luxuries, so the Mrs. stepped in and *bang*, dual income was born. To no one's surprise, women excelled, and some started to out earn their husbands, and it didn't stop there. The stay-at-home dad came into vogue and on and on. The need for man in his woman's eyes was eroding as her anger increased. He became downright less vital and a casualty of the movement through separation and divorce. A lot of men couldn't handle this new position of inferiority and either packed up or got left behind. This left Mrs. Big Bucks alone too.

> A LOT OF MEN COULDN'T HANDLE THIS NEW POSITION OF INFERIORITY AND EITHER PACKED UP OR GOT LEFT BEHIND.

Let's examine women with earning power who either leave relationships or are abandoned. It's one more divot in the fairway of togetherness. Abandonment seems a complete contradiction for women who can earn as much or more than men. You'd think all that extra cash flow would contribute to keeping a stable relationship healthy, or if it failed, the girl would be able to hook up at the drop of a hat. Yet, it's just not true. Those same women fear a decline in social standing that comes with divorce in a way men simply don't understand.

The ironic thing here is that men usually have a tougher time adjusting and are less happy after the split. But here's

> SHE FEELS BETRAYED TO HAVE TO GO OUT THERE AND KEEP MAKING MONEY AND LET THE MAN OFF THE HOOK.

the problem when the woman has been the big earner. She feels betrayed to have to go out there and keep making money and let the man off the hook. She also feels the terror of being left alone, no matter how much money she makes. This occurrence is a major driver in the whole "look like a teenager" beauty industry.

Let's look at a scenario. If a man and a woman get married, and the woman is smarter, richer, and more ambitious, is this a formula for unhappiness down the road? Should the man be relegated to play second fiddle? Would there be equality in that marriage?

Here's the kicker. Aren't both parties in this relationship committed to becoming one? If the man were the breadwinner, they'd share the workload and share the wealth with no hard feelings, yes? So what about vice versa? Apparently not!

Today's statistics show when the roles are reversed, women are not so forthcoming or happy. It seems she develops a deep-seated anger about being put into that situation. A survey by the Skipton Building Society concluded that many women who are the main breadwinners hold it against their partner. While those women might like the material rewards of their high salaries and they may outwardly say it doesn't matter, it does. (There doesn't seem to be much equality here.)

Man's logic would simply say, "Get over it" and point out that the women fell in love with him for certain reasons and he's still that man. Same thing goes for him. He would also point out that if the roles were reversed, everything would be hunky-dory. So why the meltdown? It's complicated, but I think it's safe to say that the whole equality thing hasn't quite played out yet. There's still a lot of searching for who we are in both sexes. The real question is, can women live at peace with their newfound equality, and can they live happily ever after without a loving man beside them who's not bringing in the dough? This is one damn tough question, and no one has the answers.

***

Let's talk about child-rearing in the absence of a father. Is removing the daddy from the family equation good or bad? There's no question for the majority of the population that the male child must have a role model to deal with testosterone. Daddy's the role model of how the youngster must learn the balance we've been pounding you with. So that's gotta happen. What about the other side of the coin? Let's talk specifically about Daddy's little girl.

Traditionally it is Dad who offered daughters a sense of protection and safety. Could be a throwback to the caveman days, but he affords security from the removal of nasty insects and mice to reassuring his little princess against evil things that go bump in the night. It is also from fathers that girls learn major lessons about the world of boys. Granted, they get a healthy dose of macho role model heroes and villains from TV and movies, but its Dad's interaction with normal people that teaches her the real from the fiction. Lastly, relationships between adolescent girls and their mothers are frequently strained. Fathers can act as buffers by maintaining "neutral logic" while both sides may solicit his support.

One more important thing: Development of a girl's healthy self-esteem, particularly in adolescence, also falls on Papa's

> DEVELOPMENT OF A GIRL'S HEALTHY SELF-ESTEEM, PARTICULARLY IN ADOLESCENCE, ALSO FALLS ON PAPA'S SHOULDERS.

shoulders. While the typical teenage daughter is dieting in search of the perfect female figure to attract boys, a father's positive comments may well make a difference to how she sees herself. In those pubescent days, most girls still want their father's approval, and by giving his, she gains self-confidence and self-esteem. These qualities can help her later on in life, but if they are lost, those same insecurities can cause behavioral changes, notably in health.

It seems as time marches on and our women age, eating clinics report a fourfold rise in females seeking help for anorexia and bulimia because they're desperate to look slim and youthful. Women pay big dollars for cosmetic surgery and Botox treatments, claiming they want to feel better about themselves, but unless they are homosexual or a hermit, it makes sense that these drastic measures are driven by a primeval appeal to attract or keep their men. So on the surface it looks like women still want to be around us guys.

How about family? Is man vital to that? Today we know that good fathering is imperative, as twentieth-century man has woven himself into the fiber of the family. It's definitely a feather in his cap and is a major reason why families stay cemented over time. Of course, there is no question that good child-rearing excels when both parents share in the process.

***

Let's move along to a really pertinent question. What about all that arguing between mother and father? Here's a glimpse into most men's worlds. Too many arguments have tumbled completely out of proportion from a seemingly small thing. Or, they originate from outer space. Man's logic is always butting heads with women's emotions, and most women have made their frustration clear about this polar division. They verify logic versus intuition along with rational versus emotional behaviors that do not go hand in hand. These extremes have the potential to damage any relationship. Feminists try to glorify women's "intuition" to avoid "logic." They see this "logical" trait as somehow overtly "male" (obviously a psychological problem resulting from too much testosterone, as if logic has a female and a male segment attached to it).

Quite innocently, men are often accused of being too "cold"—not because there is anything wrong with their ideas, but because they do not understand the invisible dialect (i.e., feelings) of female conversation. Just as innocently, other arguments end up on the same page because women are often accused of being "too emotional." It seems that we argue in completely different languages.

> IT SEEMS THAT WE ARGUE IN COMPLETELY DIFFERENT LANGUAGES.

When you think about it, whoever created us put both genders here for a reason. The fact is that the construction, function, and mechanics of men's brains and bodies are different than women's. That's a given! So why are we trying so hard to be the same? Add to the equation the fact that we are living way beyond the years of procreation. Doesn't it make sense that those differences should still be there and bring out the best in each?

Perhaps the goal as couples should be to grow and learn

about life with and from each other. If you plop two intelligent people into a twenty-five-year mortgage, it won't matter whether the abode is a city dwelling, a suburb, or an oceanside condo. The man is probably never going to think her way any more than she will think his. Perhaps the aim of marriage is not to think alike, but to think together and to do it without pounding each other.

I'm sure that in all long-term relationships there have been days, weeks, maybe years when the chips were down. Experiencing and growing from those struggles is what relationships are all about. As time marches on, both should realize neither is anywhere near the person they were at the beginning of the marriage. By going through all the turmoil and nurturing, we should be able to see a brighter light. Given the alternative, a couple that still shares their love despite their differences is much better off together than apart.

***

Let's do some more hypothesizing and see if girls need boys. Women in the twenty-first century may boast that they are truly independent now that equality is burning rubber in all four gears. They may tell their bosom buddies they don't need a man. They can even start a family on their own thanks to in vitro fertilization techniques. Experiments that create sperm using stem cells taken from a female's bone marrow are underway as well. In a couple of decades, this might put men on the endangered species list.

But while feminists argue that equality proves women have finally removed the shackles and dependence from men, society begs to differ. In evolutionary terms, this huge shift in cultural change amounts to a millisecond in time. No matter how powerful this change is, it will likely take the general population another ten thousand years to become logistically equal. It will take about the same time for men to achieve real emotionality, that is, if they're still around. Simply stated, whether they like it or not, most women are still genetically preprogrammed to feel dependent on men.

What about toughing it out solo? Today's emancipated women may be enjoying all the opulence of success, but statistics show that deep down in their psyche, there is fear of loneliness. As strange as it seems, when it comes to relationships, men are the glue. Here's why. Females are smaller and weaker than males. In prehistoric times women and their offspring were prone to being the victims of predators and violence. They needed support and protection, but they also needed social status, and that's why women predominately look for a mate of higher social standing.

> AS STRANGE AS IT SEEMS, WHEN IT COMES TO RELATIONSHIPS, MEN ARE THE GLUE.

In fact, modern surveys consistently show that women hunt male partners who are socially dominant. They accomplish this by observing how their potential man is respected by his peers and how he interacts with other men.

All of these ingrained rituals have been there since Adam and Eve, right? So without the need to attract a mate, would young women still be so obsessed with their physical attributes? Where would their desire to attract a mate for baby making take them? If they didn't have to woo a partner in the open market, would their flirting hormones start to atrophy?

We don't have to worry about that quite just yet. Today's premarital couples meet at speed-dating evenings, social functions, or internet connections. Typically, a young man will judge a woman on her looks and youth. His priorities are whether she's healthy, interested in sex, and able to give him children one day. He doesn't care how much she earns or her social status.

An available young women's first question will be: "What do you do for a living?" Don't be fooled by her casual demeanor. She's focused on finding out his social position and earning capacity.

As a blatant example, we've all witnessed the overweight, not-very-attractive cigar-wielding bald man who is being escorted by attractive younger women in droves. Because of his status, earning power, and willingness to hand out the dollars, he gets the babes. Put the same guy out cleaning your sewer and you know the result. Does this make women shallow? No! It's just the way it is. "Money plus power = aphrodisiac." Always has, and always will, regardless of sex.

Strangely enough, men are attracted to rich and powerful women too. What's good for the goose is good for the ganger. Hey, equality rocks!

> MONEY PLUS
> POWER =
> APHRODISIAC.

Getting back to whether men should share late-life relationships, the jury is still out. As we age and remarry or date, things change. For women, after all the kids have left the nest, they should be more stable and ready to share with a new improved partner, perhaps even have a physical relationship.

The man has matured too. He's given up looking for the young hot babe and is happy with all of those intangibles that make an older couple click. He's even come to grips with less sex. The result? Both begin to consider a twilight romance

> WHEN THIS HAPPENS, THERE'S A REAL CHANCE OF UNCLUTTERED LOVE AND ROOM FOR BOTH TO EXPRESS THEMSELVES WITH NO ULTERIOR MOTIVES.

where compatibility, care, and support are more important than the physical. The older woman exudes more independence and doesn't need as much security. Plus, the man doesn't have to go out there and break his neck earning a living. So a lot of the pressure is off.

When this happens, there's a real chance of uncluttered love and room for both to express themselves with no ulterior motives. Isn't that where we'd all like to end up? A man and a woman, side by side, sharing and caring.

So let's tell it like it is. Do young women need men? Check out the clubs, man. All that exposed skin and gyrating is happening for a reason. Furthermore, are there social climbing women out there with a pretty straight course of action aimed at successful men? Of course! Conversely, are there men who are out there just for the booty? Stupid question! We must admit, both have selfish motives, and both have a good chance at getting what they're looking for.

When you get down to the bone, women are after men just as much as men are after women. It's natural. It's the purest form of a union. Throw in for good measure most men can open a jar of pickles or wire an electrical outlet, and we must admit there are some things women will always find useful about them.

Here's a few interesting trends that show women are changing their habits over the last couple of decades. These all point to how women handle their affairs and their new autonomy. As they have become more empowered, have earned more money, and have bathed in the light of new independence, they are carving out a new niche for future female generations. Men have watched from the sidelines as some of the following preferences picked up steam.

1. Women over forty have hooked up with their girlfriends, both married and single (while hubby/boyfriend stays at home), to go on vacations, weekends at the spa, retreats, and other various excursions.

2. Divorce rates are headed down over the last twenty years. Seems as we age, infidelity becomes more tolerable. This could be due in some part to a higher rate of fooling around by women.

3. We have seen the wives of many high-profile politicians and celebrity/sports marriages forgive and forget. When there seems to be a solid base, both family and financial, the indiscretion does not rock the basic foundation. Therefore, the big picture remains the focus. The indiscretion is swept under the carpet and the relationship remains intact.

So we're back to a final question. Would the planet be better off without men? Here's a short list of scientific data that suggests men's days may be numbered:

1. SHRINKING Y CHROMOSOME

As we talked about earlier, the natural selection process is slowly eroding the Y chromosome. A typical X chromosome boasts more than a thousand genes, the Y chromosome has shrunk to just seventy-eight, leaving male babies more susceptible to genetic conditions. If the Y chromosome continues its downward spiral, it could eventually die out, marking the end of sexual reproduction forever.

2. IMMACULATE CONCEPTION

Keepers at the Henry Doorly Zoo in Omaha, Nebraska, were left scratching their heads in 2001 when one of three female bonnethead sharks gave birth by parthenogenesis (a process where an egg develops into an embryo without being fertilized) despite having had no male contact in three years. Could this evolve to women? Not in our lifetime, but it's interesting to consider.

3. FALLING SPERM COUNT

Research has proven that men's sperm counts have been falling over the generations, due to chemicals in the atmosphere and injected hormones into livestock. These have damaged both men's and women's reproductive systems. These man-made concoctions could account for the male species dying out within 125,000 years. It's also the reason why ten-year-old girls are developing breasts and pubic hair.

4. WORKPLACE EQUALITY

Now that pursuit for equality has hit the speed of light and girls are consistently outperforming boys in school, even in math and science, some believe it's only a matter of time before women overhaul the status quo. With women still doing the lion's share of domestic duties, men will become increasingly marginalized.

5. KOMODO DRAGON

One supposedly female dragon at Chester Zoo produced a batch of fertilized eggs all by herself. Later tests proved that this large lizard had been able to self-fertilize. The zoo curator was at a loss: "After she (it) gave birth, we didn't know whether to make her a cup of tea or pass out the cigars."

6. FEMALE VERSUS MALE BRAIN DEVELOPMENT

Although men on average have slightly more brain tissue,

more brain cells, and marginally higher IQs, women use their brains more succinctly. The fact is that every embryonic brain starts off female. Male characteristics only kick in around the eighth week. Once the male sex is determined, the brain produces an excess of testosterone, which shrinks the communication center, reduces the hearing cortex, and makes the part of the brain that processes sex twice as large. (So this is where it all begins, eh?) Women's brains develop with much less of the nefarious hormone. The result? Women excel at communication using twenty thousand words a day to men's seven thousand. And unlike men, unless the boys are left handed (a whole new controversial topic), they use both sides of their brain to process emotions. Huh! Go figure.

> NEW MAN IS *WORSE* THAN OLD MAN.

Here's the point of view of some women today: New man is *worse* than old man.

While he's been trying to make a living, he's lost most of his menial skills. Now, he openly cries real tears but has to pay someone to wire a plug or fix a shelf. Add the cruelest cut—he claims alimony if we leave him. Lastly, man's only contribution to housework is opening the door for the cleaning lady while he doodles with the remote.

Here's one final piece to think about. It's from Mark J. Miller's (no relation) article on Marti Barletta. She states that fifty-year-plus women are entering the best time of their lives, personally and professionally. They'll be at the top of their games for the foreseeable future. As consumers, they're affluent, upbeat, and ready to spend, but ignored by most marketers.

This is the first generation of "Prime Time Women,"

Barletta says, because their life experiences are so different than those of women who preceded them. They're the first generation to go to college in equal numbers to men; the first to work outside the home for pay in large numbers; and the first to benefit from major advances in health, fitness, and nutrition that are boosting the life expectancy of women (currently 79.5 years and rising). The result? Fifty-plus American women are the healthiest, wealthiest, most active generation of women in history.

> FIFTY-PLUS AMERICAN WOMEN ARE THE HEALTHIEST, WEALTHIEST, MOST ACTIVE GENERATION OF WOMEN IN HISTORY.

So I leave it up to the girls. Do you want to be courted by the male gender? Is there anything you gals actually like about us? If men weren't out there to mate with, where would all the chase and catch games go? Would there be a need to look so good by augmenting your breasts and lips or reducing your hips and ass? I hope both sexes can contribute to where our evolution is taking us. I'm hoping we can find a way to work together, love one another, and be happy in each other's company, so fulfillment can be attainable in later life. If we make it, we'll party all night long. The beer and martinis are on me.

Scoreboard: Let's call it a draw and leave it at that. This way we all win.

PROFOUND IMPACT

When I was fourteen, I visited my godfather, Uncle Doug, in the hospital. He was dying of cancer. I really wasn't that close to him, and he really wasn't my uncle. He was my godfather because he'd served in the Second World War alongside my dad. They had returned as best friends. In the 1950s, I guess that was enough to qualify for "godfather" status. And so it was.

I vaguely remember Uncle Doug and his wife at our house for the odd party. That was the only real contact I had with him until the day my father informed me about his deteriorating situation with cancer and that as a conscientious "godson," I should visit him. As a war veteran, it was my dad's way of passing on the message without using the D word. I felt obliged to go.

I only visited Uncle Doug twice. The first was routine enough. He looked a bit paler and quieter than usual, but no big deal. Two weeks later, the picture had drastically changed.

It was the first time in my young life that I witnessed how this disease could wither a human.

I'd brought him a magazine, as a kind of present, because I didn't know what else to bring a dying man. In fact, "dying" was a term that I, as a neophyte teenager, couldn't really get a grip on. I mean, inner discoveries like soul, past lives, future lives, or any other pre- or post-breathing phenomena were chronologically years away.

Spiritually, my sister and I were sent, not taken, to church by our parents ('cause they had spent their parentless time in church as children and were passing this rite on to us). So we were schooled as standard Roman Catholics. The nuns and priests taught us about heaven, hell, and purgatory, but in truth, all of those destinations were a stretch for me. Dying in a state of grace, by absolution, into the Kingdom of God seemed more like an immaculate reception (not to be confused by a Pittsburgh Steeler's touchdown catch in the '80s).

God's Catholic rules were not enough to scare me into not stealing or lying or a few other semi-mortal sins. In fact, religion in general was pretty bogus to me. It didn't make a lot of sense to be looking over your shoulder every time you did something pretty cool, wondering if God was there watching and shaking his finger in your direction. In fact, religion had come and gone by the time I was visiting my dying Uncle Doug.

Speaking of dying, my only recollection of even considering the mystical idea of death was when I was five and suffering with pneumatic fever. I can remember looking into the mirror, convinced that I was shrinking and surely about to die. However, within a couple of months that turned into years with regular penicillin tablets, that thought vanished like Santa and the tooth fairy, and vibrant life was again the norm. From my post-rheumatic days, I set out to see where life would lead ignoring the D word, because when you're an active healthy teenager, you're invincible.

You may have acne; your body may be a touch gangly without real definition. Your ears may grow faster than your other facial features. You may have a wanton desire to look at or, if you're lucky, touch budding female breasts, à la previous chapters. You may play a variety of sports all day and night or sip sodas at the corner chip and hot dog joint, but death is not a top ten menu item. It's not even remotely in any conversation except when adults or parents talked about funerals of old people.

That, of course, made sense. Old people die. And my uncle Doug, even though he was in his early forties (pretty much the same age as my dad), seemed pretty damn old to me and in this cancer-stricken state, even older. I was okay with that.

At his bed, inside the curtained-off room he shared with two other cancer patients, I presented my gift. He took the magazine, a *Sports Illustrated* or something related, smiled, and then dropped it on the sheets. He pulled me closer, because his voice wasn't very strong, and pointed to his wristwatch.

"I've been a working man all my life." He gurgled while he unclasped the watch from his wrist and held it up near his nose. "I've been a slave." He looked at the crystal, his hand visibly quivering, then dropped the watch onto a bedside tray and covered it with a towel. His eyes rolled back into his head while the phlegm in his throat caused his next whisper to be even raspier.

"I've spent my whole life chasing time." He seemed to be recounting every single day in his past. "I woke up to an alarm clock, punched in and out of work, got home in time to eat, then usually hit the sack by ten so I could do it all over again, day after day."

His deep-brown eyes were like two sharp daggers piercing my blue eyes, commanding my attention, and I, unaware of anything else but his words, held my gaze.

"I'm going to give you some advice," he said clearly as I felt his hand squeeze mine. "Don't ever wear a watch." His words brought me into a hypnotized state, his piercing stare evaporating everything in the room.

I waited a few seconds for something more profound while our hands and eyes were connected. I blinked a few times. I didn't feel the earth moving. "Is that it? I mean, is that your advice?" The words leaked out, barely audible. His wisdom had clearly gone over my head, because I didn't wear a watch. I was too poor to own one.

He rested his head onto the pillow and drew a deep breath. "What I really mean to say is that if you are having a good time doing something, stay. If you're having a bad time, leave and never worry about the time."

Those words hit me like a sledgehammer. Thousands of visions poured through my head. *Yeah. He's right. I should leave school right away. I could play road hockey or touch football all day and all night ... or not go to bed when my parents told me. I really didn't like sleeping anyway. I didn't want to miss anything.* The list was endless on where I should stay and where I should leave.

I noticed his hand had slipped out of mine. I looked over.

Tears were running down both his cheeks, his head slightly turned away. He was too weak to wipe the tears, way past any vanity to even care. "Forgive me," he mumbled off in another direction.

I wasn't sure if he was addressing me, God, his wife, or any number of choices, but at that moment he didn't seem so old or so sick, and I didn't seem so young or so healthy. In fact, it was my first awareness of two souls communicating on another level where words didn't matter.

IN FACT, IT WAS MY FIRST AWARENESS OF TWO SOULS COMMUNICATING ON ANOTHER LEVEL WHERE WORDS DIDN'T MATTER.

The message was instant and crystal clear. We were connecting on a higher plane. Those few seconds, as it turned out, were about to define my very existence and mold a million decisions of my future life. Looking back now, it was the inauguration of a search for "balance."

His confession about how he had spent his time on this planet doing what was expected of him, such as fighting for his country, earning a living, being responsible, and making sacrifices in the name of—well, that's one thing that wasn't clear. But the gist of his words seemed to give the impression that he felt he'd been cheated out of a fulfilled life, or maybe was upset that he wouldn't be around to be fulfilled. Either way, it was clear that most of his life was spent doing things he was supposed to do rather than what he wanted to do.

I was just a kid and had no idea about the whole concept. However, his advice had set in motion concepts that are still in my thoughts until this day. I left his room a few minutes later and said a silent goodbye, infected by his spoken word forever. I never saw him again. He was cremated, and I didn't go to the funeral.

This was my first recollection of words and thoughts which deeply impacted and altered the way I looked at life. Because of Uncle Doug, I began spending my time doing things that mattered and stayed away from or cutting time drastically on things I didn't.

I returned to my parents' home that day armed with this new direction. In line with my uncle's advice, my parents divorced after a decade plus of unhappiness using the "we're staying together for the children" excuse.

> "IF YOU'RE HAVING A GOOD TIME, STAY. IF YOU'RE HAVING A BAD TIME, LEAVE."

Ensuing freedom on all sides won out, and my sister at nineteen and I at seventeen were more than happy to be rid of all the fighting and drunkenness that permeated the matrimonial home. We set out on our own. She took a job as a flight attendant in Kansas City. I moved in with a couple of buddies and started a part-time job to pay the rent and complete my education. Every decision I made from that day on revolved around Uncle Doug's advice. These words set the tone for balance as I struggled and worked on controlling Mr. T throughout the various stages of life.

Take these words to heart and see how they impact your life.

**"If you're having a good time, stay.
If you're having a bad time, leave."**

Bottom Line and Final Wrap-Up for Testosterone and Balance:

1. Be proud to be a man.

2. Take care of your woman and family.

3. Be a role model to young people.

4. Stand up among enemies that mean you harm.

5. Work toward love and understanding.

And let the testosterone roll.

ABOUT THE AUTHOR

Regg A. (like egg with an R) Miller was born in 1950, the year of the great flood and was raised in Winnipeg, Manitoba, Canada, where he completed a science degree at the U of M. Unsatisfied with the traditional job market, he moved to Montreal, where he pursued modeling and acting. He quickly became one of Canada's top male models and moved seamlessly into television commercials, where he sold beer, cars, clothing, soap, sinus pills, and pretty much every other product on the market, as well as hosting sports television shows.

He then got behind the camera, directing and producing many corporate videos and began copywriting, where he landed several marketing opportunities for international companies. As a by-product, he lived and worked in many North American cities like New York, Los Angeles, Chicago, Vancouver, Seattle, Toronto, Miami, Dallas, Portland, Las Vegas, and many more. Internationally, he has marketed companies in Italy, Portugal, France, the UK, Germany, China, Korea, and Russia. Over his years, these opportunities and experiences have put him into contact with thousands of men and women who experienced the turmoil and sexual freedom of the '60s, the rapid explosion of female rights and technology in the '70s, and the frenetic hunt for material wealth in the '80s. It is through these decades and people that he acquired his knowledge and current point of view. As a baby boomer, he is sharing those experiences with you, the reader.

PROVOCATIVE THOUGHTS
TO CONSIDER:

"If you want to blame someone for creating men the way they are, blame God. He built the prototype and injected us with DNA and Mr. T. He's the one who ripped out a rib to create beauty, so we would compete for mating partners."

"For too long our society and strong women have told us men at point-blank, "Take it like a man," "Real men don't cry," "You call yourself a man?"—even "What kind of man are you?" The operative word "man" in all these expressions seems to put some kind of "one-dimensional thickness" on us. As if we could snap our fingers or take the "man" pill to create the perfect environment where sexual, physical, and mental equality magically appears in both sexes. We all know this will never be the case."

"Fact is, women wanted and got a fairer shot at equality. So now they die earlier of heart attacks, stress-related cancers, and all those other nasty ailments that once were reserved for men. But they also got pay hikes, respect, elevated self-esteem, and job security. So are they further ahead when you throw in the family responsibilities, dual jobs, single moms, etc.? Have all these gains made them happier or more fulfilled?"

"All men (sophisticated or heathen) know, like, and desire pampering. And most women want to show this special guy their domestic side to get the poor boy hooked. This is primitive and proof of our genetic makeup, and it's been around since the first time we stood up on two legs. Stop whining, girls. You know it's true."

"For all our hero's triumphs, casual sex starts to become mechanical whether he admits it or not. The different names, smells, the way they kiss, the questions, the idle chat, the empty promises of meeting tomorrow or follow up phone calls all starts to weigh on his consciousness. This, in fact, is when men start to imagine how marriage might be. If only they could find the perfect woman."

"Accept it or not, our men have been the acquiescing catalyst for allowing both ethnic and sexual equality in our society, so why are they suffering so much? Truth is, women have been allowed to flourish because those same men have taken up the torch and encouraged them to do their thing while backing off. A fine point? Well, check out women's freedoms and status on other continents and convince me it's not so."

"Please, men have had it all since the beginning of time. We've just got here, have only begun to feel the power, and already you're complaining? You call yourself men? Let us enjoy ourselves before you try take over like you've always done in the past. OK?!"

"No matter how tough our hombre is, he has never been able to function properly when love smitten with the physical forms of Cleopatra, Marilyn Monroe, Ursula Andress, the three Jessicas (Biel, Alba, and Simpson), Raquel Welch, Scarlett Johannson, Sophia Loren, and of course, the infamous "Pussy Galores" and "Lovey Cravesits" of the world. With all his testosterone flowing and physical superiority, it's a mental fight he can never really win."